The Epistle of

JAMES

The Epistle of

JAMES

Proven Character Through Testing

A Verse-by-Verse Commentary
by
Zane C. Hodges

Edited by
Arthur L. Farstad
and
Robert N. Wilkin

Grace Evangelical Society
Corinth, TX 76210

Dedicated to the Christians
who meet at Victor Street Bible Chapel
Dallas, Texas

The Epistle of James: Proven Character Through Testing
Copyright © 1994, 2015 Grace Evangelical Society

Third Printing

Cover Design: Shawn C. Lazar
Typesetting: Sue Broadwell

Library of Congress Cataloging-in-Publication Data

Hodges, Zane C., 1932-2008
The Epistle of James: Proven Character Through Testing/
by Zane C. Hodges
p. cm. —(The Grace New Testament Commentary)
Includes bibliographical references
ISBN 978-0-9641392-0-6
Library of Congress Catalog Card Number: 94-76756
1. Bible. N.T. James—Commentaries.
I. Bible. N.T. James. English. Hodges. 1994. II. Title. III. Series.

Unless otherwise indicated, Scripture quotations are from
The New King James Version, Copyright © 1979, 1980, 1982
by Thomas Nelson, Inc.

The Epistle of

James

Proven Character Through Testing

Contents

Introduction to the Epistle 7

Chapter 1
Respond to Trials Properly (1:1-18) 17

Chapter 2
Behave Well in Trials (1:19-20) 35

Chapter 3
Be Swift to Hear (1:21—2:26) 39

Chapter 4
Be Slow to Speak (3:1-18) 77

Chapter 5
Be Slow to Anger (4:1—5:6) 89

Chapter 6
Persevere in Trials to the End (5:7-20) 109

Abbreviations and Bibliography 123

THE EPISTLE OF JAMES

Introduction to the Epistle

The Epistle of James is a beautifully constructed Christian letter written by an author with a pastor's heart. The writer is a skilled communicator. His style is both terse and graphic, employing a wide range of effective illustrations, making it easy to believe that he also taught God's truth orally with considerable power.

An indispensable element of the NT canon, the letter's profound substance renders invalid Luther's initial evaluation of the work as a "right strawy epistle." The Book of James is the voice of a great Christian leader whose grasp of the spiritual life and of human nature is equal to any in the canon of NT Scripture. The modern Church ignores James's immensely practical admonitions at its own peril.

In every way the Epistle of James justifies the Church's historic, collective judgment that it belongs among the writings which are *given by inspiration of God* (2 Tim 3:16).

I. Authorship

The author calls himself *James, a bondservant of God and of the Lord Jesus Christ* (1:1). But which James is this?

Of the four (or five) men in the NT named *James* (Greek: *Iakōbos*, same name as Jacob in the OT), we may exclude James the father of Judas (not Iscariot; see Luke 6:16 and Acts 1:13), who is too obscure a person to be a candidate for authorship. For the same reason, we can probably eliminate James the son of Alphaeus (Matt 10:3; Acts 1:13), who may be the same person as James the Less (Matt. 27:56; Mark 15:40; Luke 24:10). James the apostle (and brother of John, the son of Zebedee) was martyred at such an early date (ca. A.D. 44; see Acts 12:2) that most scholars think it is very unlikely that he wrote the epistle.

That "James" most frequently connected with this letter is the half-brother of our Lord. If the epistle was written after the death of the apostle James (but see our discussion of date), then James the Lord's brother was the only well-known James left in the Christian church of Palestine. He might then have easily referred to himself simply and modestly as "a bondservant of God and of the Lord Jesus Christ" (1:1). It is also likely that the bearer of the epistle knew its author and would so inform the recipients wherever it was read. In addition, the tone of authority in the epistle presupposes a fairly commanding and respected figure, rather than an unknown James.

Nevertheless, many modern scholars think of the Epistle of James as pseudonymous (i.e., ascribed to James by the real, unknown author). This is an improbable point of view. Would not the unknown author have made his claim to authority clearer and more pointed by naming "James" either as "the apostle" or as "the Lord's brother"? That such a claim is not made in the letter implies that the original readers were contemporaries who knew which authoritative James this was. Pseudonymity is the common resort for incredulous scholars who readily suspect a "later writer" behind every NT book.

The internal contents of the epistle agree well with the conclusion that it was written by James the Lord's brother. These may be noted as follows:

(1) The authoritative manner of the author fits the portrait of him that we get from Acts (Acts 15:13-21; 21:18ff.).

(2) The high moral standards of the author, and especially his emphasis on prayer, are reflected in a famous reference to James the Lord's brother by the patristic writer, Hegesippus (2nd century). Eusebius (HE 2.23) quotes Hegesippus as saying that this James was distinguished from others named James by the title "the Just," and that

> He drank neither wine nor fermented liquors, and abstained from animal food. A razor never came upon his head, he never anointed with oil, and never used a [public] bath . . . He was in the habit

of entering the temple alone, and was often found upon his bended knees, and interceding for the forgiveness of the people: so that his knees became as hard as camel's, in consequence of his habitual supplication and kneeling before God.

Even supposing a measure of inaccuracy here (as is common in uninspired accounts of noble people), the basic picture is clear. The James so described must have been a man of exceptional moral rectitude, reflecting the character of the author which the epistle's contents portray.

(3) Authorship by James the Lord's brother, who rose to prominence in the Jerusalem church, is supported also by the physical notices in the epistle which point to a Palestinian situation for both readers and writer. Note: (a) the writer is not far from the sea (1:6; 3:4); (b) his land is blessed with figs, oil, and wine (3:12); (c) salt and bitter springs are known there (3:11, 12); (d) there is reference to the hot wind so common in Palestine (1:11), as well as to the former and latter rain (5:7).

(4) Although they cannot be pressed too far, there are resemblances between the Greek of the epistle and the speech of James to the Jerusalem Council. See the following cross references:

James	Acts
1:1	15:23
1:16, 19	15:25
1:27	15:14, 29
2:5	15:14, 25
2:7	15:17
5:19-20	15:19.

(5) There are also certain resemblances in James's letter to the Sermon on the Mount, which a brother of Jesus could well have heard:

James	Matthew
2:13	5:7
3:12	7:16
3:18	5:9
5:2	6:19
5:12	5:34-37.

Thus, there are no compelling grounds for setting aside the traditional view of authorship by James the Lord's brother. On the contrary, the epistle dovetails in important details with this identification of its writer.

II. Audience, Date, and Destination

James designates his intended audience as *the twelve tribes* (1:1). The phrase seems naturally to identify the recipients as Jewish. The tone and contents of the epistle agree with this. One recent writer observes that "the Jewishness of James is so pervasive that it has been used to support the position that James, the Lord's brother, wrote the epistle" (Songer, *RevExp*: 361).

At the same time, the notion that James is a non-Christian Jewish document, into which some Christian additions have been inserted, is now properly regarded as a fiction. Nevertheless, James makes no reference to the Gentiles, nor does he show any awareness of the kind of evangelism typical of the Pauline mission. This suggests the possibility that James was written at a date prior to the Gentile outreach recorded in Acts.

If the traditional date of James's death (A.D. 62) is correct, the epistle cannot have been written later than that. Instead, the absence of any concern with the issues raised by the conversion of Gentiles, suggests the possibility that the letter might be dated as early as the middle or late 30s . We may take April 3, A.D. 33 as the date of the crucifixion. (For a convincing discussion, see Maier, *ChHist*: 3-13.) The conversion of Saul of Tarsus (Paul) could have taken place in A.D. 34, leaving about a year, or a little more, for the events of Acts 1-9. In that case James could plausibly be dated as early as A.D. 34. As Robinson has noted (*Redating*, p. 121), "there is nothing in James that goes outside what is described in the first half of Acts." We may add that nothing in the epistle goes beyond Acts 1-9.

If James is regarded as quite early, before the spread of the Gospel to the Gentile world, we can understand the phrase *the*

twelve tribes which are scattered abroad accordingly. The words
scattered abroad translate the Greek words *en tē diaspora* ("in
the dispersion"). Robinson comments:

> The *diaspora* does not appear here, as in John 7.35, to be
> *contrasted* with metropolitan Judaism, nor as in I Peter 1.1, to
> stand for scattered *Christians*, many if not most of whom had
> never been Jews (cf. I Peter 2.10). Like "the twelve tribes that
> inhabit the whole world" in the Shepherd of Hermas (Sim.
> 9.17.1f), it is a way rather of describing "the whole Israel of God",
> for whose peace Paul prayed (Gal. 6.16). James is addressing all
> who form the true, spiritual Israel, wherever they are. And he can
> address them in such completely Jewish terms not because he is
> singling them out from Gentile Christians but because, as far as
> his purview is concerned, *there are no other Christians*. In Zahn's
> words, "the believing Israel constituted the entire Church"—and
> that was true only for a very limited period of Christian history
> (*Redating*, p. 122; italics original).

This is helpful. Observe, however, that the scattering of the
Jewish Christians (at the first persecution, Acts 8:1) *did*
produce a kind of Christian *diaspora* (dispersion). From their
unified, communal situation in Jerusalem (cf. Acts 4:32-35),
the early Christians were "dispersed" throughout Judea and
Samaria. In fact, in Acts 8:1, the English words *they were . . .
scattered* translate *diesparēsan*, which is from the same Greek
root as *diaspora*. If James was written to this dispersed
audience not long after they had undergone this very trou-
bling experience, the writer's pastoral stress on the spiritual
value of our trials is highly appropriate.

It is possible that the letter was written even prior to the
evangelization of Samaria. But since the Samaritans had a
racial relationship to the Jews, the early Christians could have
viewed the Samaritan converts as returning to the spiritual
community of *the twelve tribes* who constituted the true Israel
of that day (cf. Rom 2:28-29). A close study of the early
chapters of Acts shows that the Christians did not yet regard
the Church as an entity distinct from Israel in purpose and
character. That enlightenment was to come later through Paul

and through the other *holy apostles and prophets* of the early Church (Eph 3:5).

Interestingly, the letter of James contains no reference to chu₁ch leaders of the kind we would now call "pastors." Although elders are mentioned (5:14), the only reference to teaching suggests that this activity was so far from being a function reserved for certain men that James must warn his readers that *not many of you* should *become teachers* (3:1). This fact, too, fits as early a date as we might reasonably postulate.

In conclusion, therefore, we suggest that the Epistle of James was a pastoral letter written to the dispersed Jewish believers of Palestine, probably at a time *before* Paul's initial mission to the Gentile world, i.e., *to Arabia* (Gal 1:17). This would suggest a date closely approximating A.D. 34 or 35. On this view, James is by far the earliest NT document that we possess. (Galatians, the next book written, can be dated about A.D. 49).

III. Early History of the Epistle

Although the Epistle of James may have been written long before any other NT book, it probably came into general circulation much later. Indeed if, as we suggest, it was a pastoral communication from James to the scattered congregations of Palestine, it had no single destination. Rather, the bearer of the letter may have moved from congregation to congregation allowing it to be read in each assembly of believers. Whether the epistle was copied in any of these places is unknown. But it is possible that the original could have been left with the last congregation for whom it was intended.

When Palestinian believers fled from Palestine during the Jewish War with Rome (A.D. 66-70), the original—if it still existed—*probably went with them*. Alternatively, a copy or copies of the original might go abroad at that time. Hence the letter of James would become known in the wider Christian community only after the death of James himself and after the destruction of Jerusalem. Since the Palestinian church effectively ceased to exist after the Roman war, the authenticity of the letter bearing James's name was hard to verify in the very area where it had originated.

A history something like this probably explains the relatively slow reception of the Epistle of James in the larger Christian Church. The earliest Christian writer to mention the letter as the work of James the Lord's brother was Origen (ca. A.D. 254), who seems to have accepted it as Scripture. It was also accepted by Athanasius (ca. A.D. 296-373). It is absent from the Muratorian Canon, which is a fragmentary list of the books of the NT known at Rome about A.D. 200. Eusebius of Caesarea (ca. A.D. 265 – ca. A.D. 339), in his *Ecclesiastical History* (2.23), acknowledges that the epistle was disputed, that "not many of the ancients have mentioned it," but also stated that it was "publicly used in most of the churches."

J. B. Mayor (*Epistle*, p. lxx) has made the claim that "if I do not deceive myself . . . our Epistle was more widely known during the first three centuries than has been commonly supposed." His data (pp. lxix—lxxxiv) deserves attention for its overall impact, despite the opinion of many modern scholars that the resemblances to James show only that the epistle draws upon a common paraenetic tradition (i.e., material containing ethical exhortation). But Mayor's data cannot be dismissed this way without begging the question of who influenced whom. Did the paraenetic tradition influence the epistle, or did the epistle influence the paraenetic tradition? If the Epistle of James can, on other grounds, be viewed as possibly quite early, then the answer is obvious. The author of this letter is such a gifted rhetorician that his oral and written communications must surely have influenced the ethical exhortation of early Christianity.

Thus Mayor could be right, for example, that Clement of Rome, ca. A.D. 95, may have known about the epistle (*Epistle*, pp. lxx-lxxi), and this would then be the earliest surviving extrabiblical use of the letter. But if our view of the letter's history is basically correct, Clement may not have known of it before A.D. 70. In any case, he is not likely to have had a copy that was so familiar to him that he could consult it easily for verbatim quotations. (Chapter and verse divisions of the NT were still 12 and 15 centuries, respectively, in the future!) The allusive nature of his possible references to James are thus easy to understand.

In summary, therefore, there is nothing in the early history of the Epistle of James that would incline us to question its authenticity and early date. Those who find such questions in the history are usually guided by an unwarranted zeal to discover them.

IV. Literary Character

The extremely influential commentary on James by form critic Martin Dibelius (died 1947) maintained the view, still popular today, that James should be regarded as paraenesis. As previously noted, paraenesis was a form of ethical exhortation widely used in pre-Christian literature, both Jewish and Hellenistic. It was characterized by aphorisms and compact units of thought which were loosely strung together by the author—hence the term "string of pearls" to describe this form. Those who see James in this light usually give up on the idea that the epistle presents an organized development of a basic theme. (See, e.g., Songer, *RevExp:* 362-64.)

But other scholars do not accept this approach and are much more inclined than some older writers to see a thematic structure in the epistle. The insightful article in 1970 by Fred O. Francis (*ZNW:* 110-26) was something of a pioneer undertaking in terms of a structural analysis of James. Francis's outline in many places resembles the one we offer below (under VI). Among those more recent writers who perceive in James a concern with structure or development, we may mention C. B. Amphoux, Peter H. Davids, Euan Fry, A. S. Geyser, Gilberto Marconi, Ralph P. Martin, J. A. Motyer, François Vouga, and Duane F. Watson. (For their writings, see Bibliography.) It will be the premise of this commentary that the epistle *does* contain a discernible structure. The correctness of this premise must be demonstrated by the exposition itself.

It should be kept in mind that if James was written before Paul's Gentile work began, then the famous passage in 2:14-26 can hardly be an effort to refute, or correct, any form of Pauline theology. The repeated effort to relate the epistle to some kind of faith versus works controversy is misguided and has led more than one commentator into an interpretive cul-de-sac! But here, too, the final proof must rest on the cogency of our exposition of James 2.

V. Purpose

James was writing to the Christians who had been *scattered* (1:1) by the persecution that arose after Stephen's death. This persecution had probably now subsided (see Acts 9:31). No doubt the memory of their recent trouble was still fresh in the readers' minds. But enough time had passed for new difficulties to appear, and the stress these caused was manifested in various kinds of intra-church problems, such as quarrels and disputes (4:1). James's letter is an effort to encourage these believers to face trials with faith and perseverance (5:7-8, 10), and he also seeks to renew a spirit of peace within the churches (5:9).

The structure of James's letter allows us to define his purpose even more closely. The threefold admonition of 1:19, *let every man be swift to hear, slow to speak, slow to wrath*, in fact, is the key to the letter's development. James adopts for his letter a structure known and approved for speeches by ancient writers on rhetoric (see Kennedy, *Rhetorical*, p. 48; cf. Watson, *NTS*:94-97). Of course, as contemporary rhetorical criticism has pointed out, the NT documents were almost certainly intended for public reading in the churches where they went (Achtemeier, *JBL*:3-27). Thus James's letter is basically a speech or sermon, cast in written form (so Motyer, *James*, pp. 11-13). Its basic elements are as follows: a preface, or prologue (1:2-18), followed by a thematic statement (1:19-20);

a body, called by the Greek rhetoricians the *kephalaia*, or
"headings" (1:21-5:6); and an epilogue (5:7-20). The outline
below seeks to clarify this structure.

With this ground plan in mind, the thematic material in
1:19-20 permits us to see the purpose of James as set forth in
the following outline:

VI. Outline

Theme: James encourages the behavior needed in times of trial.

I. SALUTATION (1:1)

II. PROLOGUE: RESPOND TO TRIALS PROPERLY (1:2-18)
A. By Welcoming Them (1:2-11)
B. By Not Accusing God (1:12-18)

III. THEME: BEHAVE WELL IN TRIALS (1:19-20)

IV. BODY OF THE LETTER: CULTIVATE THE NECESSARY
BEHAVIOR (1:21-5:6)
A. By Being Swift to Hear (1:21-2:26)
  1. Which involves more than mere listening (1:21-27)
  2. Which involves more than mere morality (2:1-13)
  3. Which involves more than passive faith (2:14-26)
B. By Being Slow to Speak (3:1-18)
  1. Because the tongue is a dangerous instrument
  for displaying wisdom (3:1-12)
  2. Because holy conduct is a safe instrument for
  displaying wisdom (3:13-18)
C. By Being Slow to Wrath (4:1-5:6)
  1. Since wrath is created by worldliness (4:1-5)
  2. Since wrath is cured by humility (4:6-5:6)
    a. When it brings repentance from sin (4:6-10)
    b. When it brings restraint in speech (4:11-12)
    c. When it brings reluctance to boast (4:13-5:6)

V. EPILOGUE: PERSEVERE IN TRIALS TO THE END
(5:7-20)
A. Because Perseverance Will Be Properly Rewarded
(5:7-11)
B. Because Perseverance Can Be Undergirded by Prayer
(5:12-20)

CHAPTER 1

Respond to Trials Properly
(James 1:1-18)

I. SALUTATION (1:1)

¹ James, a bondservant of God and of the Lord Jesus Christ, to the twelve tribes which are scattered abroad: Greetings.

The author of the epistle was evidently James, one of the half-brothers of our Lord (see *Introduction*). He was also a prominent leader in the Jerusalem church. Yet he does not lay claim to any prestigious title at all, but simply calls himself *a bondservant of God and of the Lord Jesus Christ*. This humility might well be expected of a man who grew up in the same household with the sinless Son of God.

James addresses an audience whom he calls *the twelve tribes which are scattered abroad*. If we are right in thinking that this epistle was written to Jewish Christians not long after the first persecution of the church in Jerusalem (ca. A.D. 35; see *Introduction*), the addressees are the true *believing* Israel within the larger Jewish nation (cf. Rom 2:28-29; 9:6-8). Thus they are the true *twelve tribes* because their hearts have been *circumcised* by faith (Col 2:11-12).

In this light, the reference to the readers being *scattered abroad* (Greek: *en tē diaspora*, "in the dispersion") does not refer to the Diaspora, i.e., to the dispersion of ethnic Jews all over the Roman world that took place centuries earlier. Instead, it refers to the scattering of Jewish believers in the persecution that followed the martyrdom of Stephen (Acts 8:1). Some time had passed (a few months?) since then, and these believers had taken advantage of less stressful times (cf. Acts 9:31) and had settled into various assemblies of believers throughout Palestine. Yet, continuing pressures were felt by them because they constituted a Christian minority among their unbelieving Jewish contemporaries. James writes to them in a pastoral capacity in which his concerns are especially focused on the on-going problems and trials which they faced.

II. PROLOGUE: RESPOND TO TRIALS PROPERLY (1:2-18)

A. By Welcoming Them (1:2-11)

² My brethren, count it all joy when you fall into various trials, ³ knowing that the testing of your faith produces patience.

Naturally, James refers to his readers as his *brethren*, not because they are fellow Jews but because they have been born from above, *brought . . . forth by the word of truth* (1:18; cf. Acts 9:30; 10:23; etc.). This form of address, *(my) brethren*, is frequent in this epistle (1:16, 19; 2:1, 5, 14; 3:1, 10, 12; 4:11; 5:7, 9, 10, 12, 19). Even a superficial reading of James 1:2-18 shows that the author regards his readers as Christians. It may be said that nowhere in the letter—not even in 2:14-26!—does he betray the slightest doubt that those in his audience are truly his brothers or sisters in the Lord. If we do not observe this simple and obvious fact, we may fall into a quagmire of skewed interpretations, just as so many expositors of James have actually done.

The words *count it all joy* are really the opening words of v 2 (in Greek). They strike precisely the note of triumph that James wishes to sound for his Christian brothers. *Various trials* have occurred—and will continue to occur—in the lives of these readers. How should they face them? What attitude should they take? They should count them as *joy*, James declares. But not merely as a partial or insufficient kind of joy. Rather, James insists, they should count them as *all joy*, or (more idiomatically) as a "total joy"! How unnatural this is to the human heart is obvious. We usually greet troubles with distress and complaining! Clearly, James is exhorting these believers to view their hard times with the eye of faith.

Why should they count their trials as *all joy*? Because these trials have a positive and highly beneficial purpose in the plan of God. And that purpose is stated here as something known to the readers. God's intention in allowing our faith to be tested is to produce *patience*, more accurately, "endurance" or "perseverance." The author of Proverbs wrote, *If you faint in the day of adversity, your strength is small* (Prov 24:10). God is in the business of building up strong Christian men and women who can "persevere" in hard times without fainting.

The Greek phrase translated by the NKJV as *the testing of your faith* treats the Greek word *dokimion* as a noun. But *dokimion* could be the neuter singular of the adjective and literally can mean: "the genuine [thing] of your faith" (cf. BGD, p. 203). A comparable expression is found in the papyri in the sense of "standard [refined] gold" (see MM, pp. 167-68). We suggest the meaning, "your quality-proven faith," i.e., "your unalloyed [pure] faith." James is referring to the way trial and testing apply "fire" to our faith, so that it can come through the "furnace" of trouble cleansed of any dross or impurity from the flesh. Like gold that has been refined, faith can be purified from the selfish motives and misguided perceptions that often distort and weaken it. God can use trouble to accomplish just that.

⁴ But let patience have its perfect work, that you may be perfect and complete, lacking nothing.

But we must not be impatient. This is the thrust of v 4. When James urges his readers to allow "endurance" (*patience*, NKJV) to *have its perfect work*, he means that they should allow the Lord to accomplish a complete work of endurance within them. Too often we are so eager to escape our difficulties that we seek mere relief from the trial, rather than to gain every possible spiritual benefit from it. If we say, "I cannot endure any more of this," then God's work of endurance within us is not *perfect* (Greek: *teleios*, "complete"). We can always endure what God allows (1 Cor 10:13).

A *perfect work* of "endurance," therefore, is what we should desire the outcome of any of our trials to be. When God is "allowed" (by our submission to Him) to do such a work, then we will be *perfect and complete, lacking nothing*. Of course, by *perfect* James does not mean sinless perfection. Both of the Greek words here mean much the same thing, but we might render them this way: "that you may be complete and intact, with no deficiency." God is seeking the fully developed Christian person who (in the popular phrase) "really has it together." Such a man or woman is prepared to cope with life's adversities in deep reliance upon the sufficiency and grace of God.

⁵ If any of you lacks wisdom, let him ask of God, who gives to all liberally and without reproach, and it will be given to him.

One of the deficiencies which trouble often exposes in us is lack of wisdom. Thus, if "endurance" is to accomplish its "complete work" in us, the deficiency in our wisdom needs to be supplied. Of course, James is not speaking here of any and all wisdom, since we will always be deficient in many such areas while still in the body. Rather, in this context, James is speaking of that particular wisdom we will need in order to cope with the *various trials* we experience.

So if a particular trial exposes a particular lack of wisdom in some area, what should we do? James's answer is that we should pray for this wisdom. Then the God to whom we pray will give it *liberally and without reproach*. Both of these characteristics of divine giving are significant here. We do not need to wheedle or cajole wisdom from God. On the contrary He gives it *liberally*. That is, He loves to bestow wisdom and He bestows it bountifully. In granting wisdom our God is the very opposite of an earthly miser who may have much but is reluctant to give away anything. God does not "hoard" His wisdom, but dispenses it lavishly to *all* those who ask for it in faith (cf. v 6).

But God also gives wisdom *without reproach*. How easily He might chide us for our ignorance and stupidity—as also for how little we have learned in so long a time! But when we ask in faith, He does not *reproach* us for what we do not know. Instead, He is eager to supply our deficiency from His boundless treasure of wisdom and knowledge. *Ask*, James reiterates, *and it will be given to you* (Matt 7:7; Luke 11:9).

⁶ But let him ask in faith, with no doubting, for he who doubts is like a wave of the sea driven and tossed by the wind.

There is one stipulation, however. The request for wisdom must be made *in faith*. This also means the request must be made *with no doubting*. Faith and doubting are opposites, of course. When one doubts, he is not believing. When one believes, he is not doubting. (See Matt 14:31; 21:21; 28:17; Mark 11:23; Rom 14:23.) The Christian who comes to God for wisdom must come with calm confidence in the Lord. If his heart is buffeted by doubts about God's willingness or ability to grant the request, then this Christian *is like a wave of the sea driven and tossed by the wind*. That is, he is in the grip of uncertainty and perplexity.

⁷ For let not that man suppose that he will receive anything from   the Lord; ⁸ he is a double-minded man, unstable in all his ways.

His failure to trust the One to whom he comes in prayer is serious. Indeed, it is an insult to God Himself. Such a man should not expect to *receive anything from the Lord*. Just as our Christian life began with the confidence that eternal life was ours by faith in Christ, so our on-going need for wisdom must be sought from God with a similar confidence.

On the other hand, it must not be assumed that the answer to a prayer for wisdom will come like a bolt of lightning at the moment it is requested. Such a conclusion would ignore the context of James's thought here. James has just told us that God's goal in our trials is to furnish us with those spiritual assets which we lack (vv 3-4). Thus, we can expect God to answer our prayer for wisdom through the very trial itself, as we *endure* it until God's *perfect work* in us is done. In this light, an appropriate prayer might be: "Father, help me to gain from this trial the wisdom You want me to have."

The Christian who cannot make up his mind to leave his need for wisdom confidently in God's hands is spiritually *unstable*. He is, in fact, *double-minded* (Greek: *dipsychos*, "two-souled"). He is a kind of "split personality." One part of him knows that he must leave this need for discernment with God, while the other part still feels that he can, and must, solve the puzzle by himself. The result of such an inward division in our perspective is likely to be a zigzag course of action filled with mistakes and false starts. The Christian who combines a lack of wisdom with the spirit of a "doubting Thomas" is a prime candidate to make a mess of things. Or, as James puts it, he is *unstable in all his ways*.

⁹ Let the lowly brother glory in his exaltation, ¹⁰ but the rich in his humiliation, because as a flower of the field he will pass away.

James now returns to the leading theme of his prologue, namely, the proper attitude toward our *various trials* (vv 2-3). The proper attitude is joy, since God uses trials to bring about our spiritual maturity. Verse 4 has counseled patience in the face of trials so that God could fill up our deficiencies. Verses 5-8 have been a brief parenthetical discussion on asking for wisdom.

Verses 9-11 are often interpreted as though they were unrelated to the flow of thought in the preceding verses. For example, Mayor (*Epistle*, p. 44) connects *glory*, v 9, with *all joy*, v 2, without making the obvious link to *trials*. However, the verses are actually and directly related to the leading idea of the passage, which is, "Accept trials in the proper way." Citing the word "brother," Mitton (*Epistle*, p. 33) correctly observes, "The paragraph clearly applies to Christian people."

How then should *the lowly brother* accept trials? (By a *lowly brother* James probably means a "poor brother," since he is contrasted with *the rich* [brother] in v 10.) Does not a

Christian of low estate in life have enough problems just by virtue of his status? How can such a *brother* calmly, indeed joyfully, accept the additional trials which often befall him, especially those arising from the very fact of his being a Christian? James's solution is simple. That brother should consider his trials a form of *exaltation*!

But, again, how can this be? Two reasons are suggested in the immediate context. First, God is paying attention to *the lowly brother* by using trials to make him a better person (vv 3-4). There is no higher honor than to be the object of God's gracious and loving concern. Equally, God is preparing to bestow on this brother *the crown of life* which comes to those who endure testing (v 12 and discussion). That too is an *exaltation*. Thus the lowly brother's *exaltation* is both present (in the trial itself) and prospective (in the trial's outcome). This, then, should be the poor person's perspective on trouble.

It is different for the *rich* brother. (We should certainly supply the term "brother" here, since it is clearly implied by the contrast with v 9 and by the general flow of thought.) The wealthy Christian brother should *glory* (also implied from v 9) in his personal trials as a form of *humiliation*. Like all people with abundant material wealth, the wealthy Christian can easily forget that *as a flower of the field he will pass away*.

[11] For no sooner has the sun risen with a burning heat than it withers the grass; its flower falls, and its beautiful appearance perishes. So the rich man also will fade away in his pursuits.

Trials, however, can be used by God to remind the rich Christian of the transience of his own earthly life and of how quickly all his material belongings can be lost (cf. Luke 12:16-21). He should rejoice in his sufferings because they humble him and because, after all, he is a mere human being whose life is a *vapor that appears for a little time and then vanishes away* (Jas 4:14).

To underline his point, James here compares the wealthy man to mere *grass* of the field whose *flower* (blossom) *withers* under *burning heat*. His *pursuits* (activities) will abruptly cease when he dies! The rich Christian can take occasion from his troubles to be reminded of all this.

In other words, in his *various trials*, the wealthy believer should say to God: "Thanks, I needed that!"

B. By Not Accusing God (1:12-18)

¹² Blessed is the man who endures temptation; for when he has been approved, he will receive the crown of life which the Lord has promised to those who love Him.

With this verse, James begins the second unit of his introduction (or prologue). The twofold (doubled) character of this introduction was observed in 1970 in an important article by Fred O. Francis. He noted, for example, that "the main argumentative interests of the epistle are introduced in carefully balanced thematic statements (1:2-11 and 1:12-25)" (ZNW: 118). Although we believe that the second unit ends with v 18, Francis's observation can stand. It may be noted that the main difference between the two subunits is that vv 2-11 stress the proper attitude toward suffering itself, while vv 12-18 stress the proper attitude toward God in these sufferings. The note of loving God is struck for the first time in v 12.

Suppose, then, that every Christian, rich or poor, takes the attitude prescribed for him by James in vv 2-11, what then? James's answer is that, the person who *endures temptation* can anticipate a *crown of life*.

The choice of the word *temptation* here (in the NKJV) tends to obscure the connection of this verse with what precedes. The Greek word rendered *temptation* (*peirasmos*) is the same one translated *trials* in v 2. (The concept of being tempted to evil becomes appropriate only with v 13.) James is here building on his discussion (vv 2-11) of the proper attitude for times of trial (see also the discussion of *those who love Him* later in this verse). Obviously, if we are to *endure* trials to their proper end, joyful acceptance of God's will should play a crucial role. If our eyes are fixed on the beneficial goal of trials, then in this very outlook we adopt an attitude of faith and submission to the Lord, which facilitates endurance.

Thus, when the trial ends and *when* the believer who endures it *has been* (Greek: *genomenos*, has become) *approved*, there is a reward. In using the word *approved* (*dokimos*), James is alluding to the character development he has referred to in vv 2-4. Paul's thoughts in Rom 5:3-4a are similar: *And not only that, but we also glory in tribulations, knowing that tribulation produces perseverance* (cf. Jas 1:3); *and perseverance, character* (Greek: *dokimēn*, "approvedness"). Thus, the divinely desired result of our troubles is approved character. The man whose endurance through trial has cooperated to produce this outcome is indeed *blessed* of God.

So why should he be considered *blessed* (i.e., "happy," or "fortunate")? The answer is that (since he has become approved) *he will receive the crown of life*.

The question arises here as to whether *the crown of life*, to which James refers, is a present benefit or a future one. Either view is possible, but the *life* in question must not be confused with the free gift of life that James mentions shortly (vv 17-18; cf. Rom 6:23; Rev 22:17; etc.). Clearly, here in v 12, we are looking at a *reward* for enduring our trials.

If a *future* reward is in view, a parallel verse might be Gal 6:8, where the future "harvest" of our deeds is presented as the reaping of *everlasting life*. Although eternal life must be received initially as a gift, the possibility of having it *more abundantly* (John 10:10) is held out to obedient Christians. James could have this concept in view.[1]

It seems much more likely, however, that James has in mind the way God enriches our *present* experience of life, when testing has been successfully endured. This interpretation takes on a high probability when we recall James's later statement in 5:11: *Indeed we count them blessed who endure. You have heard of the perseverance of Job and seen the end intended by the Lord—that the Lord is very compassionate and merciful.* Obviously this statement picks up the themes of 1:3-12, including the reference to being *blessed* (1:12) in the words "*count . . . blessed*" (5:11). Every Jewish-Christian reader of James would know how God had crowned Job's life with blessings after his trials were over. Therefore, it seems quite likely that it is the enrichment of our *temporal* experience of *life* (spiritually always, materially sometimes) that James has in mind in the expression *the crown of life*. Life will be richer, deeper, fuller for his Christian readers if they are among those who, like Job, reach the end of their trials victoriously. Indeed, every time we successfully endure a period of trouble, *the crown of life* will be awarded to us anew. In this respect, as in others, *the path of the just is like the shining sun, that shines ever brighter unto the perfect day* (Prov 4:18).

Finally, this experience is for *those who love Him* (that is, the Lord). To such and only to such has God *promised* this *crown of life*. In fact, it may be stated that each of our *various trials* in some way or other is a test of our love for God. With each test there comes the temptation to resist God's will in sending the trial at all or, at least, the temptation to resent it and thus refuse to allow God to do the character-building work He desires to perform in us. Only when we submit lovingly to God's mighty hand do we find *the crown of life* awaiting us at the end of the trial. *Those who love Him* are the very ones who discover that *weeping may endure for a night, but joy comes in the morning* (Ps 30:5).

¹³ Let no one say when he is tempted, "I am tempted by God"; for God cannot be tempted by evil, nor does He Himself tempt anyone.

This new subject of love for God (v 12) now leads James to discuss a new aspect of our attitude toward trials. In these trials, what is our attitude toward *God*?

If a Christian does *not* love God, a wrong attitude toward testing can easily arise. The idea that all Christians *do* love God is a fiction. Even our Lord felt it necessary to exhort His inner circle of eleven disciples on this point (cf. John 14:21-24). Judas, it should be remembered, was already gone, and Jesus' audience consisted only of born-again men. In no circumstances more than in trials does the presence or absence of love for God in a Christian become more apparent.

The crown of life, therefore, is for *those who love Him*, but *not* for those who accuse God of tempting them with evil.

At this point in his prologue, James has made a subtle shift in his use of the word *peirasmos* from its broader meaning of "trial" or "testing" (vv 2-12) to its more narrow meaning of "temptation" or "solicitation to evil." It may be safely said that in every "trial" (broad sense) which we have, there is also a "temptation" to evil (narrow sense).

Such was the case with Job. The calamities which overtook him (Job 1:13-19) were his "trial," but the "temptation" involved Satan's aim to induce Job to *curse God* for his difficulties (Job 1:11; 2:5, 9). Job *endured* his trials and *resisted* the temptation that came with them. In like manner, whatever our particular type of trouble, there invariably comes with it some solicitation to do or say the wrong thing— perhaps even the temptation to curse God for our sorrows.

In fact, one of the temptations we may face in times of trial is the temptation to blame God for the inward inclination toward evil which usually surfaces under stress. If we love God properly (1:12), we will never say that these evil inclinations are *His* responsibility. The person who claims, *"I am tempted by God,"* has forgotten that *God cannot be tempted by evil, nor does He . . . tempt anyone.* Instead, the source of our temptations is the inward pull exerted by our *own* [evil] *desires.* If we were not evil people we would have no such desires and would be free of wrong impulses.

The question arises, then, how could Christ Himself be tempted if *God* cannot be tempted? Was not Jesus *God?* He most emphatically was and is. And unlike ourselves, His human nature was totally free from the slightest evil impulse or inclination. Yet there is no real problem.

We must recall that the concept of temptation is both objective and subjective. When someone tries to persuade us to do wrong, he is, *objectively* speaking, tempting us. He is soliciting from us an evil word or deed. But at the same time, *subjectively* speaking, we may not actually be "tempted," since all his efforts may not awaken in us any desire to do the particular evil he suggests. Someone might easily say: "He *tempted* me to break the law in as many ways as he could think up, but lawbreaking scares me and does not *tempt* me at all!"

So too, the Lord Jesus Christ was truly "tempted" by Satan because Satan exerted great efforts to seduce Him to violate God's will. But the Lord was *not* "tempted" by any of these efforts, since His perfectly holy nature contained nothing that could respond positively to Satan's solicitations. Thus it was as true of Jesus on earth, as it is of God at any time, that (as James says) He *cannot be tempted by evil*.

¹⁴ But each one is tempted when he is drawn away by his own desires and enticed.

Clearly, then, in this passage James is thinking of "temptation" in the subjective sense. All Satan's efforts to lead people into evil, and all of the world's seductions, would have no effect on a person at all unless *he is drawn away by his own desires and enticed*. In the final analysis James is right. There is no temptation for us except when we respond to some seduction in an inward way and find the evil in some way desirable.

It is worth noting that James affirms of God that *He Himself* does not tempt anyone. This means that God is not *personally* the agent of temptation, but James's words leave room for the truth that God *allows others* to engage in temptation. Again, Job is the classic example. God *Himself* did not tempt Job, but He *allowed* Satan to do so.

Thus the readers of James's letter must not sinfully charge God with responsibility for their temptations. Rather, the responsibility is their own because of their own wicked hearts.

¹⁵ Then, when desire has conceived, it gives birth to sin; and sin, when it is full-grown, brings forth death.

James now goes on to trace the potentially deadly consequences into which man's evil desires can lead him. The language he employs is the language of childbearing. *Desire* (as if it were a woman) experiences a "conception" (*syllabousa:* when [desire] has conceived) and subsequently *gives birth* (*tiktei*) *to sin*.

If we analyze the experience of temptation, James's words are instructive. Desire, he says, is the mother of sin. Perhaps we might even suggest that such conception occurs when desire, or lust, is united with the human will, so that the birth of sin becomes a determination of the heart. But after the sin is brought to birth through lust, it grows (or, is repeated) and reaches maturity (i.e., *when it is full-grown*). Then sin in turn bears a child of its own—namely, *death* (*sin . . . brings forth* [*apokyō*: "gives birth to"] *death*).

Death, then, is the grandchild of sinful lust or *desire!* Death is the cul-de-sac into which our lusts can lead us. This point is reaffirmed by James in 5:20: *He who turns a sinner from the error of his way will save a soul from death.* The truth that physical death is the ultimate end of sinful conduct is stated repeatedly in the Book of Proverbs (e.g., 10:27; 11:19, 12:28; 13:14; 19:16). Since James is writing to his Christian brothers (see discussion of 1:2), it is plain that even a born-again Christian can flirt with premature physical death by indulging his sinful lusts. This is an extremely serious consideration.

But immediate repentance from sin, that is, a turning from the error of our way (5:20), can cut the sin off before it is *full-grown* and thus save the sinning one *from death.*

¹⁶ Do not be deceived, my beloved brethren.

So James's Christian brothers and sisters should not allow themselves to *be deceived.* How could his readers ever imagine that God had tempted them? Temptation to evil can lead to physical death, and death is the very opposite of the kind of gift that God always bestows. In fact, death is the dreadful consequence *earned* by our sins (Rom 6:23), while our God is fundamentally a *Giver*.

¹⁷ Every good gift and every perfect gift is from above, and comes down from the Father of lights, with whom there is no variation or shadow of turning.

Indeed, He is a flawless Giver, unlike all earthly givers. *Every good and perfect gift* is from Him and therefore *from above*. We might have expected James to say that God only gives *good and perfect* gifts, but in fact he says more than this. Wherever there is such a thing as a flawless gift, that gift is necessarily *from above*. All human gifts, by contrast, are flawed in some way because the human giver is flawed. Only God can give *perfect* gifts.

That is because He is *the Father of lights, with whom there is no variation or shadow of turning.* The Greek words for *variation* (*parallagē*) and *turning* (*tropēs*) seem to have had technical uses related to the movements and changes in the heavenly bodies, i.e., in the sun, moon, and stars. This suggests that the title *Father of lights* is a reference to God as the Creator of the heavenly bodies, or *lights* (see Gen 1:14-19). But unlike these celestial bodies which undergo "variations" and cast "shadows" on earth because of their rotation in space (*turning*), God is immutable in His activity of giving.

The Creator is therefore greater than His creation. When He gives, there is no fluctuation in the quality of His gifts. They are always *good and perfect*. Moreover, no shadow of imperfection is cast by these gifts, in contrast, for example, to the shadows created by the rising or setting sun. It is unthinkable that the shadow of death (the fruit of sin) should in any way mar our experience as a result of the divine Giver's gracious bestowals upon man.

¹⁸ Of His own will He brought us forth by the word of truth, that we might be a kind of firstfruits of His creatures.

Christians should know this truth (v 17) best of all, and James's readers *are* Christians. Therefore James can say of them and of himself, *Of His own will He brought us forth*, i.e., He "gave birth" to us.

We must not miss the connection of this statement with the context. James's word for *brought us forth* (*apokyō*) is the same word used in v 15 for "brings forth." Sin, James is saying, "gives birth" to death, but God "gives birth" to *us!* Of course James has in mind here the truth of new birth and, like every NT writer, he knows it to be a *gift!* (Davids, *Commentary*, p. 89, regards "the reference to the gospel and regeneration" as certain.) Thus, following the statements of v 17 about God's flawless giving, James is using new birth as the example *par excellence* of a *good and perfect gift!* (See Motyer, *Message*, p. 57.) Expositors frequently overlook the obvious theological implications of James's thought here. To James, new birth is a gift of God (so Mitton, *Epistle*, pp. 55-61). Moreover, it is not related to the "will" of man, by which it could be flawed due to the corruption of that "will." Rather, new birth finds its source in *God's* will (*of His own will*) and is effected by *the word of truth*.

We are reminded by James's words of the statement of Paul: *For it is the God who commanded light to shine out of darkness, who has shone in our hearts to give the light of the knowledge of the glory of God in the face of Jesus Christ* (2 Cor 4:6). (Motyer, *Message*, pp. 59-60, also relates v 18 to 2 Cor 4:6.) As James's and Paul's words reveal—and as both Luther and Calvin understood—faith is not an act of the human will, but rather a firm conviction about the truth of God when we are illuminated by it. Thus Paul can describe Abraham's justifying faith as *being fully convinced that what He [God] had promised He was also able to perform*, and he adds *it was accounted to him for righteousness* (Rom 4:21-22).

God's role, then, in our conversion may be described as revelatory. As an act of *His own will* He commands the light of the Gospel to shine into our hearts so that we can perceive that light in faith. As our Lord said to Peter after his great confession, *"Flesh and blood has not revealed this to you, but My Father who is in heaven"* (Matt 16:17). This, of course, in no way diminishes man's responsibility to seek God and the illumination He alone can give (Acts 17:26-27; Heb 11:6).

Thus the teaching that goes by the name of "Lordship Salvation" is flawed at its core. By insisting that saving faith is an act of the will, it demolishes the biblical concept of faith as an essentially passive and assured reception of God's truth. Biblical saving faith is a conviction or persuasion about what God says to us in the Gospel (Rom 4:21). There is no place here for man's will—even as influenced by God's Spirit. God commands the light of His Word to shine into our hearts and, like blind men suddenly able to see, we perceive it as truth (2 Cor 4:6). Once received as truth, i.e., believed, there is no room for man's will to act. Faith and regeneration have already occurred.

Obviously, in the great affirmation James makes in this verse, there is not so much as even a hint that good works somehow are related to the free gift of new birth. Good works cannot be performed apart from man's will. It is an evasion of this common-sense fact to say that good works are produced in us by God and that God enables us to *will* to do them. For even when stated like this, the human will is active despite the fact that it is acted upon by God. In new birth, however, as James states here, God's will is active through the Word; our response is simply the passive one of confident and assured perception of the truth of the Gospel. God speaks and we believe.

The result of this amazing act of God's will and Word is that we who are born again become *a kind of firstfruits of His creatures*. The NKJV translation *that we might be* is slightly ambiguous just as is the original Greek behind it (*eis to einai hēmas*). The Greek phrase can indicate either *purpose* or *result*. If the idea were one of *purpose*, James could be saying: "God has regenerated us so that we may afterwards be (become) . . ." If the idea is *result*, then the words suggest: "God has regenerated us so that we are (already) a kind of firstfruits . . ." The latter idea seems much more natural since it gives cohesion to James's statement by making clear what we are as a result of God's regenerating activity. In addition, here we seem to meet the Pauline idea that as children of God we are a sort of anticipation or foreshadowing of what God will accomplish for the entire creation (Rom 8:19-21). It is also noteworthy that the kingdom age is described by our Lord as *the regeneration (palingenesia,* Matt 19:28), a word only found elsewhere in the NT in the famous passage on new birth in Titus 3:5.

So understood, James's point will be that God's gift of new life is so *good* and *perfect* that when we possess that life we are a foreshadowing of what God will do for all *His creatures* (all created things). Just as the first crops from a field *(firstfruits)* suggest the quality of the harvest as a whole, so the miracle of regeneration in our lives is so wonderful that what God plans for the entire creation can also be called a *regeneration* (Matt 19:28). Although James recognizes that the analogy is not exact (we are a *kind of firstfruits),* yet it carries his point effectively. There is no flaw in the gift of new life; otherwise it could serve as no true model of what God wants to do for the entire creation.

This concludes James's discussion which began at v 13. The readers should never charge God with tempting them, since temptation has its fruit in sin and death (vv 13-15). Such results cannot be God's work, and the readers would be *deceived* if they thought so (v 16). Instead, every excellent gift is what God bestows and the supreme example of this is the new life (in contrast with *death)* which He has granted to us (vv 17-18). Indeed, God's gift of life to us is a foretaste of the world to come (v 18b). If James's readers love God (cf. v 12), this is how they will view things during their times of trial.

What is the practical application of all this to the behavior of the readers? How can they best confront the times of testing that enter their lives? The writer has already told them to face these times with joy (vv 2-12) and to avoid blaming their temptations on God (vv 13-18). But what precise lines of behavior serve best under stressful circumstances?

James will now address this question.

ENDNOTES

[1] See my discussion of Gal 6:8 in *The Gospel Under Siege*, 2nd ed. (Dallas: Redención Viva, 1992), pp. 86-89.

CHAPTER 2

Behave Well in Trials

(James 1:19-20)

III. THEME: BEHAVE WELL IN TRIALS
(1:19-20)

¹⁹ So then, my beloved brethren, let every man be swift to hear, slow to speak, slow to wrath; ²⁰ for the wrath of man does not produce the righteousness of God.

James now states his answer to the question of how best to behave under stressful circumstances. The words *so then*[1] show the connection with what has been previously said. There is a sense in which we ought to describe the statements of vv 19-20 as thematic for the entire epistle. Although the advice they contain is certainly good advice for all times and situations, the exhortations of James have a very special suitability for those who are undergoing trial and testing.

His admonitions are three.

The first admonition is: (1) *Be swift to hear.* A willingness to listen properly is an essential ingredient in successful endurance under testing. Although we need this trait at all times, yet when we experience stress we urgently need to be attentive to the wisdom that God offers us through His Word or through the counsel of others based on that Word.

But typically we are more eager to *talk* in times of stress than to *listen.* Hence the second admonition is: (2) *Be . . . slow to speak.* Our eagerness to pour out our thoughts and feelings under trial needs to be restrained. As has often been said, one cannot learn anything while talking! It might even be pointed out that Job's triumph under trial was enhanced by his brief but meaningful statements in Job 1 and 2 (1:21; 2:10). It was only when he decided to engage his so-called friends in extended dialogue that the sharpness of his victory over trial was diluted. If the Book of Job had ended with chapter 2, Job would not later have needed to say, *"Behold, I am vile, what shall I answer You? I lay my hand over my mouth"* (Job 40:4; see v 5), and, *"I have uttered what I did not understand, things too wonderful for me, which I did not know"* (Job 42:3). It is a good practice for everyone who is under stress to cover his mouth—i.e., to be *slow to speak.*

The third admonition is: (3) *Be . . . slow to wrath.* Everyone knows that *wrath* (Greek: *orgē*, anger) is one of mankind's most common reactions to difficult times. The human heart is easily swayed to anger by undesirable events. Then we begin to blame men, or even God, for our troubles. Obviously the ability to avoid anger at such times is a supremely admirable trait.

But such restraint is not merely admirable; it is also functional. *For,* adds James, *the wrath of man does not produce the righteousness of God.* The ultimate goal for a Christian undergoing trial is the realization of God's *righteousness* in his life. That is to say, the moral improvement we can gain through trials, which James has already referred to (vv 2-4), is in the last analysis a growth in righteousness and God-likeness. A similar thought is expressed by the writer of Hebrews: *Now no chastening seems to be joyful for the present, but painful; nevertheless, afterward it yields the peaceable fruit of righteousness to those who have been trained by it* (Heb 12:11). Obviously, human wrath is counterproductive under trials if the goal of those trials is a righteousness that promotes inward and outward peace (see Jas 3:17-18).

It should be noted, however, that James does not forbid *all* wrath but he exhorts us to be *slow* to make this response. (Not all wrath, or anger, is sinful: Eph 4:26.) The hair-trigger temper that is set off rapidly and without restraint is decidedly *the wrath of man*—in contrast to God's own holy wrath. This kind of anger blocks, or severely inhibits, the production of *the righteousness of God* in our lives.

Finally, in the three practical exhortations just covered, we can also see the basic structure around which James builds the body of his letter. The outline which we give for James (see *Introduction*) falls naturally into three divisions related to each of the admonitions and in the precise sequence in which the admonitions occur in v 19.

In the Roman age the main body of a speech or discourse was called the *kephalaia* (headings) by the Greek rhetoricians (Kennedy, *Rhetorical*, p. 48). Thus what James actually presents in v 19 is an outline of the *kephalaia*, or topics, he will now discuss. There is little reason to doubt that vv 19-20 not only conclude the prologue but actually anticipate the contents of the main unit of the epistle. Briefly, the subject of the Epistle of James is testing, and its theme is the proper behavior under testing. Such behavior consists of eagerness to listen, reluctance to talk, and restraint in the expression of anger.

ENDNOTES

[1] The words *so then* (v 19) in the NKJV are replaced by phrases like, "this you know" (NASB) and "take note of this" (NIV) in most modern translations. The translation difference is due to an underlying difference in the Greek text that is being translated. The NKJV translates *hōste* which is found in the great majority of the surviving Greek manuscripts of James. NASB, NIV, and others translate the word *iste*, found in several ancient manuscripts from Egypt and in a small number of later manuscripts. There is a difference of only one letter between the two forms in Greek (the h in the English transliteration of *hōste* represents a "rough breathing" mark and not a letter). Either form could have been derived from the other by a copyist's error. But the error is more likely to have produced *iste* since this reading is stylistically harsh here in Greek and coheres poorly with the flow of thought. Were it not found in the Egyptian manuscripts which are greatly preferred by many at the present time, it would have been quickly dismissed as an obvious scribal mistake.

CHAPTER 3

Be Swift to Hear

(*James 1:21—2:26*)

IV. BODY OF THE LETTER: CULTIVATE THE NECESSARY BEHAVIOR (1:21-5:6)

A. By Being Swift to Hear (1:21—2:26)

1. Which involves more than mere listening (1:21-27)

²¹ Therefore lay aside all filthiness and overflow of wickedness, and receive with meekness the implanted word, which is able to save your souls.

Now that the theme of the epistle has been summarized by James (vv 19-20), the inspired author launches into an extended exposition of his theme. We have called this exposition the "body" (the main unit) of the letter. The word *therefore* (Greek, *dio*) signals the new point of departure. It is not enough for the writer simply to state the demands of v 19. He must also examine their ramifications. How easily a reader might claim, "Of course I am quick to hear God's Word!" But James's exposition puts this claim to the test.

To begin with, the believer who wishes to *receive . . . the implanted word* must prepare himself both negatively and positively. Negatively, he should *lay aside all filthiness and overflow of wickedness*. Positively, he should *receive* (or, "welcome" [*dexasthe*]) that Word in the proper spirit: *with meekness*. (Dibelius, *James*, p. 112, points out the contrast between "meekness," v 21, and "anger," v 20.)

James's statement is remarkably parallel to Peter's: *Therefore, laying aside all malice, all deceit, hypocrisy, envy, and all evil speaking, as newborn babes, desire the pure milk of the word, that you may grow thereby* (1 Pet 2:1-2). Since not all Christians of those days were sufficiently literate to read the Scriptures, both Peter and James are no doubt thinking of the Christian meetings where God's Word was read and taught. As teachers themselves for a time in the same church at Jerusalem, both James and Peter knew that the Word could only have its full effect if the hearers heard it with a right attitude. They should, therefore, repent of any sin that defiled them and adopt the meek, child-like openness to God's truth that was appropriate. This is James's point here.

The necessary preparation for "hearing" the Word, then, included the need for James's readers to divest themselves of evil. (The word translated *laying aside* [*apotithēmi*] was often used of removing clothing.) The evil itself is described as *all filthiness* (i.e., everything dirty) and as an *overflow of wickedness*. This latter phrase has been much discussed, but the most suitable rendering in context seems to be "the excrescence which evil is." (The genitive of *kakia* may be taken as epexegetical, i.e., explanatory.) That is, James calls "evil" (or, *wickedness*) an excess (*perisseia*), a kind of unwanted enlargement, or abnormal outgrowth, in the Christian's life. It is in no way probable that James means that not all *wickedness*, but only its *overflow*, should be put away by the believer who is about to hear the Word. Instead, for those whom God has *brought . . . forth by the word of truth* any and all evil is an ugly superfluity similar, for example, to an unsightly tumor growing out of a person's skin. All human evil should be renounced by the Christian before he hears God's Word.

That Word, James notes in passing, is *implanted* (*emphytos*: "inborn"). In context, it is reasonable to take this as a reference to the readers' new birth (v 18), which was effected by *the word of truth*. Like a seed *implanted* within them, the Word had imparted new life to them. It was thus an "inborn" Word which was natural and innate to them as born-again people. (See Peter's use of the *seed* imagery for new birth: 1 Pet 1:23-25.) Now these Christians should receive the instruction of God's Word, recognizing it as the very thing that had been *implanted* in them by the Gospel. It may be suggested that just as a seed of wheat contains within itself all of the potential from which fully developed wheat may grow, so too does the Gospel. Simple though the message of salvation is, the seed of life which is implanted when we believe this message contains enormous potential which only Christian obedience can fully develop. Thus the Word we *hear* in Christian instruction is nothing less than what has been *implanted* or "inborn," with all its potentialities, within every believer.

Furthermore, *the implanted word* can produce an enormous benefit, for James tells his readers that it *is able to save your souls*. Many readers as well as expositors have an automatic reaction to the phrase *save your souls* in English, which leads them to understand it of eternal salvation from hell. But none of James's readers were at all likely to get such a meaning out of this text. The Greek phrase found here (*sōsai tas psychas hymōn*) was in common use in the sense of "to save the life." It is used in both the Greek OT as well as in the NT in exactly that sense (see Gen 19:17; 32:30; 1 Sam 19:11; Jer 48:6; Mark 3:4//Luke 6:9). This is its obvious sense also in Jas 5:20, which refers to the physical preservation of a life *from death*. It may even be said that there is not a single place in the entire Greek Bible (i.e., the NT plus the Septuagint, the Greek translation of the OT) where this phrase signifies deliverance from hell. (For the Lord's metaphor using this phrase, see the discussions at Matt 16:24-28; Mark 8:34-38; Luke 9:23-27.)

It is unfortunate that most interpreters of James are either unaware of this data or dismiss it as irrelevant. Whenever linguistic evidence of this type is ignored, faulty interpretation is almost inevitable. Nevertheless the meaning which the data supports—"to save your lives"—is precisely the meaning most suited to this context. The readers are already born again (v 18) and are in no need of being saved from hell. Moreover, James has just spoken of the death-dealing consequences of sin (vv 14-15). In this light, the meaning of v 21 is transparent: although sin can culminate in physical death, the Word of

God, properly received, can preserve physical life. This thought is deeply embedded in the wisdom literature of the OT in statements like these:

> "The fear of the Lord prolongs days,
> But the years of the wicked will be shortened"
> (Prov 10:27).

> "As righteousness leads to life,
> So he who pursues evil
>   pursues it to his own death"
> (Prov 11:19).

See also Prov 12:28; 13:14; 19:16.

From both a linguistic and contextual point of view, as well as from the perspective of Hebrew wisdom, there can be no legitimate doubt about James's meaning in this verse. To take these words as a reference to eternal salvation is to commit an obvious error of eisegesis (reading one's own ideas into the text). As long as a reader does that in v 21, he will not only misunderstand the verse itself, but he will misunderstand the entire epistle, including 2:14-26!

²² But be doers of the word, and not hearers only, deceiving yourselves.

As important as it is to *receive the implanted word* with cleansed hearts and a meek spirit, there is one further essential step. One must *do* God's Word. James's readers must never allow themselves to become mere auditors of the Word; instead they must obey it. Here, of course, James trades on the fact that the word *hear*, in both Hebrew and Greek, can mean either mere sensory audition, or it can mean also "to hear responsively," i.e., "to obey" (see BGD, *akouō*, 4). In his exposition of the command to *be swift to hear* (v 19), James wants his audience to realize that the regular hearing of God's Word in the meetings of the church is not all he has in mind. To *be swift to hear*, at its deepest level of meaning, means also "to be swift to obey." If the readers ever thought that mere attention to the Scriptures was enough, they were mistaken.

With such a view they would be *deceiving* themselves. The analogy today would be the Christian who is fascinated by the exposition and study of God's Word but who has assimilated very little of it into everyday life.

²³ For if anyone is a hearer of the word and not a doer, he is like a man observing his natural face in a mirror; ²⁴ for he observes himself, goes away, and immediately forgets what kind of man he was.

James goes on to point out, in fact, that hearing the Word without doing it is like looking into a mirror and then forgetting what one has seen. As L. T. Johnson has pointed out in his article, "The Mirror of Remembrance" (*CBQ*:632-45), the "mirror" was used in Hellenistic ethical teaching as a common metaphor for moral instruction. A hearer or reader of the epistle who was familiar with this convention in his day would find James's words especially meaningful. Johnson observes, "The man who goes away and forgets what he looks like is immediately recognizable as the one who has not properly used a mirror for self-improvement by turning 'hearing' into 'deeds'" (*CBQ*:640).

What is seen in this mirror is described by James as *his natural face* (*to prosōpon tēs geneseōs autou*). A more precise rendering of the phrase would be "the face of his birth." In the word "birth" (*geneseōs*) we can hear, as we did in the word "inborn" (v 21), a further echo of the readers' experience of regeneration (v 18). "The implanted [inborn] *word*" (God's mirror: 2 Cor 3:18) reveals to its Christian hearers the true "face" of their new birth into God's family. It shows them what they truly are *in Christ* and, therefore, how they *ought to behave* in keeping with that image of themselves.

Needless to say, this approach to Christian morality is a fundamental feature of the NT epistles. We begin by recognizing what we are by God's grace, and we are then commanded to behave *accordingly*. One can discover this principle, among many other places, in such texts as Rom 6:5-14; 1 Cor 6:15 and 19-20; Gal 2:20; Eph 4:1; Col 3:1-4; 2 Pet 1:3-7. Thus the believer who hears the Word, but goes out and ignores what it has shown him, is truly like a person who *immediately forgets what kind of man* he is. To be a mere hearer of God's truth is to forget our true identity as born-again and justified children of God, and to behave as though we were not.

²⁵ But he who looks into the perfect law of liberty and continues in it, and is not a forgetful hearer but a doer of the work, this one will be blessed in what he does.

By contrast with such a person is the Christian who is not a *forgetful hearer but a doer of the work.* The NKJV's addition of *the* in front of *work* is a decision by the translators (there is no article in the Greek) which does not seem entirely appropriate here. To English speakers, *the work* can suggest a particular, specific work. The Greek (*poiētēs ergou*) is no doubt more general in the sense of a "work-doer." This is James's first reference to good works. It stands here in the first of a series of sections which lead up to 2:14-26.

The "work-doer" James is describing is introduced in this verse as someone *who looks into the perfect law of liberty.* The *perfect law of liberty* is the spiritual "mirror" into which a believer looks when he hears "the implanted word." Since the commands of this Christian *law* are in accord with his inner-most nature as a born-again person, they are not in any way a form of bondage but rather they are a *law of liberty* [freedom]. What the Christian really learns from the Word (as we have pointed out in vv 23-24) is to *become* (in conduct) what he already *is* by virtue of his regenerate nature. When I am doing something as a natural expression of my true nature, I am obviously enjoying the *liberty* of just being myself.

No one should suppose that James would disagree in the slightest with the Pauline teaching that we *are not under law but under grace* (Rom 6:14). Nor would he disagree with Peter that the OT law was *a yoke . . . which neither our fathers nor we are able to bear* (Acts 15:10). In fact, James's concept of the Christian life as a *law of liberty* implicitly sets it in contrast with the OT law and is very analogous to Paul's statement that we are to *fulfill the law of Christ* (Gal 6:2).

The OT law was a yoke of bondage precisely because it could not change the heart to which it was addressed. It could impart no inward, spiritual incentive to obey it, though it might produce fear and guilt. This leads Paul to affirm that *the letter kills, but the Spirit gives life* (2 Cor 3:6). Thus the OT law was fundamentally a *ministry of death* (2 Cor 3:7). Righteousness could never come by the law (Gal 3:21). But under the New Covenant (see Heb 8) God works *from the inside out*. He regenerates the sinner by His Word (James 1:18), thereby making that Word an *implanted*, or inborn, Word to which it is natural for the Christian to respond positively (*for I delight in the law of God according to the inward man*: Rom 7:22). Therefore, being a Christian involves being dead to the OT law and being married to a risen Savior and Lord (Rom 7:4-6). This means that now our service to God is carried on in *the newness of the Spirit, not in the oldness of the letter* (Rom 7:6). Such an experience of life is indeed an obedience to God's commands, but it is lived in the experience of the freedom of the Spirit. This life is now an obedience to the commands of the *New Covenant* and thus an obedience to what is truly a *law of liberty*. (See Mitton's valuable discussion in *Epistle*, pp. 71-74.)

So the Christian man who *looks into . . . and continues in* God's Word is a man who submits to divine authority (law), yet in so doing finds himself truly free. Indeed, we could easily suspect that James had personally heard our Lord say, *"If you abide in My word, you are My disciples indeed. And you shall know the truth, and the truth shall make you free"* (John 8:31-32). Such truly free obedience to God is the secret of "saving our lives" (v 21) and of enjoying every other benefit God chooses to bestow on our Christian experience. The *doer of . . . work* (or, "work-doer") of this verse, not the mere hearer of the Word, is exactly the person *who will be blessed in what he does*.

²⁶ If anyone among you thinks he is religious, and does not bridle his tongue but deceives his own heart, this one's religion is useless.

The church or churches to which James was writing (see *Introduction*) were much less than perfect (see chap 4). They probably contained many individuals who considered themselves to be punctilious in their *religious* observances and thus worthy of the blessing James had just spoken about (v 25). But it is commonplace for people to reduce obedience to God to the performance of various religious routines. In James's day these might include regular attendance at Christian worship, as well as prayers and fasting. The words for *religious* (here) and *religion* (v 27) were terms suited to describe just such activities as these. But James is not concerned with the practice of religious exercises, however valuable they are in their place. Instead, he is concerned with down-to-earth conduct in relation to other people.

Thus, *anyone* among his readers who would have labeled himself *religious* was only deceiving *his own heart* if he did not actually *bridle his tongue* when he talked to others. This comment by James certainly anticipates his extended discussion of the tongue in chap 3. But at the same time there is as much "work" involved in bridling (holding in check) our tongues as there is in reining in real horses—perhaps more! The man who succeeds in doing this to a significant degree (no one does it perfectly) has performed a good work. Moreover, much evil would be prevented if we were more proficient in this work (see 3:5-12), since our overall self-control is enhanced by controlling the tongue (3:2). James totally dismisses the *religion* of any Christian person who placed no restraint on the use of his own tongue. Sanctimonious prayers in public or private were worth little if the person who offered them had lips filled with slander, deceit, and cursing when he talked to other people (see 3:9-10).

²⁷ Pure and undefiled religion before God and the Father is this: to visit orphans and widows in their trouble, and to keep oneself unspotted from the world.

Equally, any claim to being *religious* was dashed to the ground by a failure to help the needy, or by any sinful practice derived from the unbelieving world around them. *Pure and undefiled religion* was far more than a few basic liturgical routines. The *God and the Father* of James's readers—the *Father of lights* who had regenerated them (vv 17-18)—looked for more than such routines. What expressed His nature and character best was mercy and personal moral purity. This meant James's readers needed *to visit orphans and widows in their trouble, and to keep* themselves *unspotted from the world.*

It should be noted that in the phrase *and to keep oneself unspotted from the world* the NKJV prints the word *and* in italics. This means there is nothing in the Greek text which it directly translates. Actually, it is perhaps preferable to translate the phrase "*in order to keep* oneself unspotted from the world." This would suggest that the regular practice of mercy toward orphans and widows, indeed *to visit* (Greek: *episkeptesthai*) them for their assistance, is a safeguard against worldly defilement. Any Christian who fails to mingle with and assist those who have greater material needs than his own is in serious danger of being infected by the world's selfishness, greed, and indifference. No amount of prayer and church attendance can compensate for the loss of compassion and involvement with the poor. Charity to the poor channeled in an impersonal way through the government or other institutions is not at all the same thing.

Thus James here (and in the following chapter) expresses his strong sympathy and concern for the poor. In this he reflects the spirit of our Lord Himself, who declared that He had come to *preach the gospel to the poor* (Luke 4:18) and who touched the lives of many poor people during His earthly life. For the Christian, this Christlike quality is essential to *pure and undefiled religion.*

JAMES 2

2. Which involves more than mere morality (2:1-13)

¹ My brethren, do not hold the faith of our Lord Jesus Christ, the Lord of glory, with partiality.

In developing the theme of being *swift to hear* (see 1:19), James has now pointed out that *to hear* is more than merely listening to the Word. It also involves *doing* it as well (1:21-25); yet not simply in the sense of the observance of ceremonial routines but with acts of mercy to those in need (1:26-27). Such acts guard one against worldly "spots" (1:27). It is this last point that forms a bridge to the next unit (2:1-13).

One worldly spot to be diligently avoided is that of *partiality*. Deference to the rich and disdain for the poor have always been features of worldliness, so James insists that such discrimination against the poor is unworthy of *the faith* which his readers have in *our Lord Jesus Christ*. This is all the more true because Christ is *the Lord of glory*.

Actually in this verse the italicized words (in the NKJV), *the Lord*, are not present in the original, which simply has "of (the) glory." It is possible that this latter phrase is used like an adjective in the sense of "our glorious Lord Jesus Christ." But the presence of the definite article (*tēs*) does not easily fit this view. More likely, the phrase in Greek equals "(the) Glory," that is, heaven or the presence of God (cf. 1 Tim 3:16). The whole expression will then mean "of our Lord Jesus Christ of (from) Glory." James would be thinking, in that case, of the fact that the true abode of the Lord was (and is) the glorious abode of God Himself. Such a splendid origin for Christ makes any kind of earthly wealth and glory appear drab and worthless by comparison. Faith in One who belongs to "Glory" makes all deference to rich people on earth look shabby and cheap. The readers should not combine their faith with such demeaning behavior.

[2] For if there should come into your assembly a man with gold rings, in fine apparel, and there should also come in a poor man in filthy clothes, [3] and you pay attention to the one wearing the fine clothes and say to him, "You sit here in a good place," and say to the poor man, "You stand there," or, "Sit here at my footstool,"

With the vividness of a preacher, James describes the sharply different treatments which an impressively attired rich man might receive, when he visited a Christian *assembly*, as over against a dirty-looking *poor man*. The former would be offered a comfortable seat, the latter an insignificant seat or no seat at all. Perhaps James had actually witnessed such cases of blatant *partiality* (v 1).

The idea, first suggested by Ward (*HTR*: 87-97), that a "church-court" scene is in view here is improbable. Though often adopted by commentators today (e.g., Davids, *Commentary*, p. 109; Martin, *James*, pp. 57-58), it involves a highly questionable transference of a Jewish practice into a Christian context without any clear NT or early Christian support.

Although the Greek word for *assembly* is the one used for a synagogue, the word had a broader use in the sense of "place of assembly" or even "meeting" (BGD, *synagōgē*, 2b and 5). "Meeting" seems most natural here. In fact, it has been maintained recently that the use of the word *synagōgē* for a *place* of meeting "began to develop primarily in the later first century," but that the earlier meaning referred to a group which gathered for a religious purpose (Kee, *NTS*: 281-83). In the circle of churches to which James writes (see *Introduction*), it is not likely that there were many which met in the local synagogue, since that would imply the conversion of most of the synagogue's members. Most probably the Jewish-Christian churches of Palestine met in private homes where rooms might be set aside to accommodate these gatherings. The statement, *sit here at my footstool*, is literally, "sit here under (or, below) my footstool." There could be a touch of ironic exaggeration in these words: James suggests that the position given the poor visitor is so demeaning as to be *underneath* the footstool on which the speaker rested his own feet!

However, the scene James had in mind may well have been one in which the Christians were reclining at a table to observe the Lord's Supper. If so, the rich visitor is allowed to sit down on a seat in the room to observe the proceedings. The poor visitor, on the other hand, is told simply either to stand (against the wall?) or to sit on the floor "under" (i.e., behind) the pillow or object on which the speaker placed his feet. For the concept of visitors at a Christian gathering, see 1 Cor 14:23-25.

⁴ have you not shown partiality among yourselves, and become judges with evil thoughts?

But those who behave with such outrageous favoritism are to be firmly censured. "If you do this," James is saying, *have you not shown partiality among yourselves...?* This may indeed be the meaning of the text, but it seems too obvious a conclusion to be drawn from the glaring example presented in vv 2-3. The original words (*ou diekrithēte en heautois*) can also be understood in the sense "have you not discriminated among yourselves" (see Davids, *Commentary*, p. 110). In that case, the *partiality* is condemned because it draws an unchristian distinction between the rich and the poor man. It implies that those who so behave have judged the rich man to be better and more worthy as a person than the poor man. But such judgments are morally wrong and make those who exercise them *judges with evil thoughts.*

⁵ Listen, my beloved brethren: Has God not chosen the poor of this world to be rich in faith and heirs of the kingdom which He promised to those who love Him?

The type of behavior just criticized represented a serious miscalculation. James wants to call his fellow Christians' attention to this miscalculation in no uncertain terms: *Listen, my beloved brethren*, i.e., "Pay attention to this!" The fundamental principle James now states amounts to telling his readers that partiality toward the rich flies directly into the face of reality. The despised poor man may actually be rich in God's sight, since *God has chosen the poor of this world to be rich in faith*.

More than once Scripture commends faith which is either abundant or exceptional in character (Matt 8:10; 15:28; Acts 6:5; 11:24; Hebrews 11). It is clear that not everyone who has faith can be described as *rich in faith*. Yet even a small amount of faith can have significant results (Matt 17:20//Luke 17:6). The issue here is not at all the issue of eternal salvation. Simple faith in Christ is sufficient to save (Acts 16:31). The issue rather is: How *much* do we trust God in our daily lives? How high can our trust rise when outward appearances are deeply discouraging? Ironically, a rich Christian may have less opportunity to trust God for his needs than a poor man who must trust Him day by day, and sometimes meal by meal. Thus, by the providential arrangement of God, a poor Christian may become very rich in the area of personal faith in God, while the rich Christian may be poverty-stricken in this aspect of spiritual experience. James's readers needed to remember this whenever a scruffy, poor brother came to their assembly. Despite outward appearances, he might be a spiritual millionaire!

Indeed, if so, he was also one of the *heirs of the kingdom*. By this phrase James indicates that the poor man who is *rich in faith* will be a co-ruler with Christ over the kingdom of God. Just as Christ inherits the kingdom (Ps 2:8-9) due to His loyalty to God the Father (Heb 1:8-9, quoting Ps 45:6-7), so will the co-heirs of His kingdom (2 Tim 2:12; Rev 2:26-28). Thus *the kingdom* has been *promised to those who love* God. Although salvation is freely bestowed at the moment we exercise simple trust in Christ for eternal life, the kingdom is not *inherited* that way. Heirship in the kingdom requires us to love God, which we can express only through obedience to Him (John 14:21-24), while obedience itself is the product of living by faith (see Gal 2:20). Anyone who does not live this kind of life cannot rightly be called *rich in faith*, even though he or she has believed in Christ for eternal salvation.[1]

⁶ But you have dishonored the poor man. Do not the rich oppress you and drag you into the courts? ⁷ Do they not blaspheme that noble name by which you are called?

Poor believers, then, tended to live such lives and to be people of importance in the light of God's coming kingdom, and disdainful treatment of a poor person who attended a meeting was a failure to take that fact into account. "You should have honored him," James is saying, *but* instead *you have dishonored the poor man.* Conversely, as a class, rich people were more likely to be the enemies of Christianity and to be oppressors rather than helpers of the Christian community. Though some indeed would be saved, their tendency to trust riches rather than God made their salvation difficult (Mark 10:23-27). Like ungainly camels, they were too big and self-important to enter the kingdom by simple, child-like trust. Still worse, in the Jewish context of this book, many unbelieving, wealthy Jews were a source of oppression to Christians and might *drag* them *into the courts* on any pretext. Moreover, many did not hesitate to *blaspheme that noble name by which you are called.* That is, they blasphemed the Lord Jesus Christ (see v 1). By putting the statements about rich men in question form, James is simply making them face what they already knew. It made no sense for any reader of James to obsequiously extend himself in welcoming a rich person into the Christian assembly, while at the same time slighting a potential heir of the kingdom!

⁸ If you really fulfill the royal law according to the Scripture, "You shall love your neighbor as yourself," you do well;

The failure to avoid *partiality* (v 1) in dealing with the rich and the poor was more than a failure to face reality in regard to these two classes of men. More fundamentally, it was a breakdown in Christian morality. It was a violation of Scripture's *royal law* commanding love for our neighbor based on how we ourselves would wish to be treated. Certainly no one desired to be slighted in the way described by James (v 3).

In calling the command to *love your neighbor as yourself* a *royal law*, James has created a memorable expression with more than one significant facet. The command to love is *royal* because it is issued by the King—our Lord Himself, in fact, first as the divine Revealer (Lev 19:1, 18) and then in His incarnation among men (Matt 22:37-40). But it is also *royal* because it is conduct of a high order that is worthy of a king. No doubt James is alluding to the theme of heirship in the kingdom which he had just mentioned (2:5). The heirs were the future kings of God's kingdom, and they should conduct themselves according to the *royal* (kingly) *law* of love for one's neighbor. Note how skillfully James pulls together in 2:5-9 the two great commands of OT revelation—i.e., love for God and love for man (see Mark 12:28-31). These two commands are also part of the New Covenant *law of liberty* (see discussion at 1:25 and below at 2:9). The aspiring future kings will possess (reign over) the kingdom if they *love God* (v 5), but this requires also *love for men* (this verse; see 1 John 4:20-21).

Thus, James is saying, if the readers *really* *(mentoi)* *do* fulfill the command to love others as they love themselves, they are doing the right thing (i.e., *you do well*). And they are acting in a royal way.

⁹ but if you show partiality, you commit sin, and are convicted by the law as transgressors.

But *do* they indeed fulfill it? Not if they *show partiality* to the rich over the poor, for in that case they *commit sin,* and the biblical command to love exposes them as *transgressors* of God's *law.* No doubt, as Jewish converts to Christianity, James's readers still held the moral standards of God's OT law in high esteem, as should we. After all, every one of the ten commandments, except the one about the Sabbath day, is repeated in the NT. Thus the repeated commands are binding on those who live under the New Covenant rather than under the Old, which has been set aside (see Hebrews 8). Therefore, the failure to love a brother as oneself (which is a failure reflected in *partiality*) constitutes a genuine infraction of God's will for us.

¹⁰ For whoever shall keep the whole law, and yet stumble in one point, he is guilty of all.

Furthermore, such failure exposes our inadequacy in the light of God's holy standards. An infraction of the law of the sort James is discussing is to break the law as a whole. No matter how well we might keep the rest of it, a sin against love constitutes a person a lawbreaker—i.e., a criminal before the bar of justice!

¹¹ For He who said, "Do not commit adultery," also said, "Do not murder." Now if you do not commit adultery, but you do murder, you have become a transgressor of the law.

This disturbing point is driven home by James with the observation that the commands against *adultery* and *murder* are part of the same law. Since both sins were punishable by death under the Old Covenant, James's argument has great force. Obviously, he is saying, *if you do not commit adultery, but you do murder*, your innocence in one area does not excuse you in the other. As James's readers would know, murderers suffered the ultimate penalty for lawbreaking whether or not they had ever committed adultery.

Naturally James is addressing himself to Jewish Christian readers (see *Introduction*) who still retained a high opinion of law-keeping, though possibly not as intensely as those in Jerusalem who were so *zealous for the law* (Acts 21:20). Their culture and heritage strongly inclined them to this, even after they had been justified by faith in Christ. James writes with considerable perception to such readers. Even though justification is not the issue here, his readership (like their unsaved but self-righteous fellow countrymen) put a high premium upon avoiding such sins as adultery and murder. But they needed to be reminded that a failure to love a poor brother who came to their assembly nullified any pride they might have in obeying God's law in other respects. One either obeyed it *all*, or he did *not* obey it—whatever the specific infraction might be. (For references to the unity of the law in

Jewish writings, consult Davids, *Commentary*, p. 116.)

Even today the Church readily lapses into a quasi-Roman Catholic view of "mortal" and "venial" sins. Some sins (like adultery or murder) are considered too serious to be committed by Christians, while others (like jealousy, selfish ambition, envy, etc.) are condemned but tolerated. Yet all are listed as *works of the flesh* in Gal 5:19-21. Although we can speak at times of some sins being worse than others (see John 19:11), James's words remind us that in the final analysis any sin is enormously serious because it breaks God's law and makes a person a lawbreaker.

The words of vv 10-11 could easily have been written by the apostle Paul himself. Certainly they powerfully reinforce the Pauline declaration that *by the deeds of the law no flesh will be justified in His sight* (Rom 3:20). How *could* a man ever hope to be justified by the law if, as James declares, *whoever shall keep the whole law, and yet stumble in one point, he is guilty of all?* Not even Paul could be more Pauline than that! Thus, if anyone still hopes for justification by works *before God*, he cannot derive that hope from the Epistle of James. In the modern evangelical world, it is amazing how often the statements of Paul and James about the law are readily ignored. Instead, we are supposed to believe (according to some) that we can keep God's law *well enough* to essentially validate our own conversion and so be regarded as Christian people. But such a view is Pharisaism revisited. It is not NT doctrine at all.

Even James's converted readers, however, needed to be reminded of this truth about the law, so that they would not ignore their own unloving *partiality* and carelessly regard themselves as law keepers in God's sight. "Don't think that way at all," James is saying, "for your loveless behavior sets you under the law's condemnation, not the law's approval!" Thus the kind of "hearing" James wants of his readers (see 1:19 ff.) is not mere moral separation from sins like *adultery* and *murder*. No indeed. To *be swift to hear* is also to be swift to *love*, and *that* excludes *partiality*.

It should be noted how James can effectively use the *law* in an exhortation to Christian readers who esteemed it highly. Just as Paul did, James employs it for the condemnation of sin, since *by the law is the knowledge of sin* (Rom 3:20). Thus James uses the law "lawfully," in accord with Paul's own perception of this. The law, Paul would later affirm, can be lawfully used to reprove whatever *is contrary to sound doctrine, according to the glorious gospel of the blessed God* (see 1 Tim 1:8-11). That is exactly what James is doing in this passage.

¹²So speak and so do as those who will be judged by the law of liberty.

But it is not the OT law by which Christians will be judged, but rather *by the law of liberty* to which he has already referred (1:25 and see discussion there). The qualifying phrase *of liberty* clearly suggests a differentiation from the mere term *law* when not so qualified. James certainly concurred with Peter's description of the OT law as *a yoke of bondage* (Acts 15:10), and James joined in the final solution of the law problem which was hammered out at the Jerusalem Council (Acts 15:13-29). James knows that Christians are *not under law but under grace* (Rom 6:14). That is to say, he knows that Christians are not under the Mosaic Law of the Old Covenant. But James also knows that God's will was extensively revealed for New Covenant people through the NT apostles and prophets and—above all—through "our Lord Jesus Christ from Glory." It is precisely this revelation which was made for born-again people and which appeals to the fundamental instincts of their regenerate nature. As such it is not a burden at all (1 John 5:3-5), but rather it allows them to express what they really are as children of God. Thus it is a law of freedom.

Yet at the same time it is the code of conduct by which our Christian lives will be judged. Thus we should *so speak and so do* with that fact in mind. Our Christian lives will be assessed in the light of the high and holy standards of the *law of liberty*.

In speaking of judgment, of course, James can only mean what we refer to as the Judgment Seat of Christ (see 2 Cor 5:9-11 and other texts). In reference to eternal life the believer *shall not come into judgment* (John 5:24). There is no such thing as a judgment for the believer to determine whether he goes to heaven or hell. The believer has *already* passed from death to life and no charge can be brought against him because he is *already* justified (see John 5:24; Rom 8:32-33). Those who here read out of James a doctrine of judgment pertaining to eternal life for believers can only do so by first reading it in!

Somewhat different is the view of Gale Heide (*GTJ*: 82) that James is appealing to the readers "to act *as if* [italics added] they were to be judged by the law of liberty [2:12] . . . In the instance of 2:13, James is referring to this law and the judgment that pertains to it, likely eschatological." Further on she adds, "James does not say that they will necessarily be judged by the law he has referred to . . ." (*GTJ*: 88). Heide's unwillingness to acknowledge a reference to a "new law" by which Christians will be assessed at the Judgment Seat of Christ leads her to the improbable conclusion that the readers *might not* experience the judgment of 2:12-13. The words *hōs . . . mellontes* are not naturally read in the sense "*as if* you were going to be . . ." The correct sense is that the readers *will be* judged at this judgment (Judgment Seat of Christ), as is indicated by the major translations. For example, note the NIV: "Speak and act as those who *are going to be judged* by the law that gives freedom" (italics added).

¹³ For judgment is without mercy to the one who has shown no mercy. Mercy triumphs over judgment.

Such is the solemnity of the Judgment Seat of Christ, however, that no man can view it without sensing how awesome and exacting it must be. Paul also sensed this feature of it (2 Cor 5:11). Any reasonable person must know that a judgment of his Christian life "by the book" (i.e., with full strictness) is likely to leave him with much censure from his Savior and with much loss of potential reward. What is needed in that day is *mercy*—a willingness on the part of our Lord and Judge to assess our words and deeds with the fullest possible measure of compassion. But how can we store up the mercy which will be so urgently needed in that day?

James's answer is simple and thrilling: he commends mercy. For if *the one who has shown no mercy* will experience none in that day, the converse must certainly be true: the one who has shown much mercy will experience much. Indeed, the mercy we show to others can actually "win the day" at that future experience of judgment, for *mercy triumphs over judgment*. The word *triumphs* (*katakauchaomai*) could be rendered "exults over," as if mercy could celebrate with words its victory over judgment. Hence, if a Christian constantly tempers his words and deeds with mercy, he can emerge a victor in the day of divine assessment.

In this light, then, the cold indifference toward the poor man of vv 2-3 was a dangerous procedure to follow. Instead, that poor man should have been welcomed with the warmth and sensitivity which the merciful person is careful to express. Only in that way would their treatment of him be a positive, rather than a negative, factor at the Judgment Seat of Christ.

3. Which involves more than passive faith (2:14-26)

The theme of this famous unit of James's epistle has already appeared in his letter. As far back as 1:21, James had urged his readers to receive God's Word because of its lifesaving power. This Word is able to save your lives, James had stated (see discussion at 1:21). But James quickly went on to insist that to benefit from the Word that way, one must be a work-doer (v 25; see vv 22-25). In a sense, the remainder of the unit, which clarifies the command to *be swift to hear*, explains what it means to be a work-doer (as stated in v 25). Thus a real work-doer is not simply punctilious about performing his religious routines, but restrains his tongue and is helpful to widows and orphans (1:26-27). Moreover, a work-doer is not a merely moral person, abstaining from things like adultery and murder, but is one who fulfills *the royal law* of love even toward the poor man who visits the Christian assembly (2:1-13). But this leads to a third consideration.

One cannot expect to benefit from the lifesaving capacity of God's Word if he dismisses the idea of works as though they were irrelevant. In that case, it does not matter that he is orthodox in his beliefs. Yet how easy it would be to downgrade works in a church where it was understood that justification before God was by faith alone. If God had accepted them eternally on the basis of faith, apart from works, why could He not accept their Christian lives on the basis of their correct beliefs—their orthodoxy—apart from works? This question might easily be raised, moreover, by someone who felt convicted by his lack of concern for, or by his prejudice against, the poor. As a shrewd and observant shepherd, James understood such defense mechanisms and seeks to address this one in 2:14-26.

But what James is *not addressing* is the issue of the eternal destiny of his readership. Although this famous passage is often taken that way, this approach actually rips James's text out of the larger context in which it is found. It introduces into the text a concern which James did not have here at all, and ignores the fact that James regards his readers as his brothers and sisters (1:2 and *passim*) and as born again (1:18). To get the subject wrong, of course, is to misunderstand James's *entire text* and to create a false theology about which James knew nothing at all. If this sounds too strong, it is not. The damage done to the Christian Church by an incorrect understanding of James 2:14-26 has been incalculable. It is also utterly deplorable because it betrays superficial thought and study, not only of the passage itself, but also of the entire epistle.

¹⁴ What does it profit, my brethren, if someone says he has faith but does not have works? Can faith save him?

James opens this section of admonition by confronting the fundamental issue. Suppose that someone lays claim to faith yet he cannot point to acts of obedience of the kind James has been discussing (1:26—2:13), what then? Can he expect his faith in God's Word to "save his life" (1:21) if he is not a work-doer (1:25)? In other words, *Can faith save him?*

Actually the question (in Greek) implies its own answer and might better be translated, "Faith can't save him, can it?" The expected response is, "No, it can't!" But, of course, faith *can* and *does* save when we are speaking of *eternal* salvation (e.g., Eph 2:8-9). But here—as James makes plain—faith *cannot* save under the conditions he has in mind (see discussion at 1:21).

Thus in James 2, the writer plainly makes works a condition for salvation. The failure to admit this is the chief source of the problems supposedly arising from this passage for most evangelicals.[2] We ought to start by admitting it. *And we ought then to admit that James cannot be discussing salvation BY GRACE!* But instead of admitting these points, many interpreters dodge them.

This is frequently done by trying to translate the question, "Can faith save him?" (2:14), by "Can *that* [or, *such*] faith save him?" But the introduction of words like "that" or "such" as qualifiers for "faith" is really an evasion of the text. The Greek does not really support this sort of translation.

Nevertheless, support for the renderings "such faith" or "that faith" is usually said to be found in the presence of the Greek definite article with the word "faith." But in this very passage, the definite article also occurs with "faith" in vv 17, 18, 20, 22, and 26. (In v 22, the reference is to Abraham's faith!) In none of these places are the words "such" or "that" proposed as natural translations. As is well known, the Greek language, like Spanish and French, often employed the definite article with abstract nouns (like faith, love, hope, etc.) where English cannot do so. In such cases we leave the Greek article untranslated. The attempt to single out 2:14 for specialized treatment carries its own refutation on its face. It must be classed as a *truly desperate* effort to support an insupportable interpretation.[3]

James's statements cannot be willed away. As clearly as language can express it, faith by itself does not "save," according to James. But "save" in what sense? Or, better, "save" from what? From eternal hell? Or from something else?

(Commentators err when they assume, rather than demonstrate, their answer.) The only appropriate answer, *in the light of the whole epistle*, is to say that James is picking up the theme of 1:21 (re-expressed also in 5:19-20). This theme is the truth that obedience to God's Word can "save" the life from the deadly outcome of sin (see 1:15 and discussion). Faith alone cannot do this. Works of obedience are completely indispensable.

Some who hold a view of James 2 similar to the one we are presenting here have tried to connect 2:14 with 2:13. They argue that the salvation in view is salvation from an unfavorable review at the Judgment Seat of Christ, accompanied by loss of reward (but not of *eternal* salvation). But this is not a probable connection for the following reasons: (1) James does not suggest, or even hint, that there is some form of salvation available at the Judgment Seat. He speaks exclusively of receiving a merciful judgment or an unmerciful one. (2) James *does* speak in his epistle of salvation of the *life*, not only at 1:21 but also in 5:19-20. The probability is high that James is picking up a theme he expects his readers to recognize from a previous reference to it, rather than referring to an idea not articulated at all in the letter. (3) If the flow of argument from 1:21 through 2:14ff is kept in mind, the reference back to the key exhortation of the unit (1:21) is quite natural. (4) The theme of "saving" connected with "good works" is such a compelling link between James 1:21-25 and 2:14-26, that it cannot be explained away. In fact, on reflection, the subject matter in 2:14-26 is simply an elaboration of the principles laid down in 1:21-25, as the exposition to follow seeks to show.

[15] If a brother or sister is naked and destitute of daily food, [16] and one of you says to them, "Depart in peace, be warmed and filled," but you do not give them the things which are needed for the body, what does it profit?

If we keep in mind the concept of "saving the life by obedience," we can then hear the words of 2:15-17 in a fresh light: Can the fact that a person holds correct beliefs and is orthodox "save" him from the deadly consequences of sin? Of course not! The very thought is absurd. That is like giving your best wishes to a destitute brother or sister when what he or she *really* needs is food and clothing (2:15-16). It is utterly fruitless! As a matter of fact, this kind of callous conduct on the part of one Christian toward another is precisely what James has been warning against (see 1:27; 2:2-6)! It superbly illustrates his point.

¹⁷ Thus also faith by itself, if it does not have works, is dead.

Such idle words are as *dead* (ineffectual) as a non-working faith! So James says, *Thus also faith by itself, if it does not have works, is dead.*

It needs to be carefully considered why James chose the term *dead* to describe a faith that is not working. Yet the moment we relate this term to the plainly expressed concept of "saving the life" (1:21), everything becomes clear. The issue that concerns James is an issue of *life* or *death*. Can a faith that is dead save the Christian from *death*? The question answers itself. The choice of the adjective *dead* is perfectly suited to James's argument. Just as the idle words of some ungenerous believer cannot save his brother from death in the absence of life's necessities, no more can a non-working faith save *our* lives from the *death-dealing* consequences of sin. For that purpose faith is sterile and ineffective *by itself*, because it cannot accomplish the needed result.

Commentators often deal with the word *dead* very simplistically. As a metaphor, *dead* is often treated as though it could refer to nothing other than the death/life terminology employed to describe salvation from hell. But every linguist knows that "death" and "deadness" are concepts that have given rise to numerous and diverse metaphors in nearly every language. English itself has many ("this law's a dead letter," "you're dead wrong," "he's dead drunk," "he's a dead duck," "that idea is dead," "they navigated by dead reckoning," etc.). So also the Greek language (and the NT itself) abounds in such metaphors. Thus, in Romans alone, Paul can call Abraham's body *dead* while it was still alive, and can attribute "deadness" to Sarah's barren womb (Rom 4:19). He can say that *apart from the law sin was* [or is] *dead* (Rom 7:8; although sin can be quite active apart from the law: Rom 5:13), and then declare that *sin revived and I died* (Rom 7:9). So too the Christian's body, in which the Spirit dwells, can be described as *dead* (Rom 8:10), although the Christian himself is regenerated. The complexity in Paul's use of the term *dead* is clearly evident from these texts. A concordance study will yield examples in other parts of the NT as well (e.g., Luke 15:24, 32; Heb 6:1; 9:14; Rev 3:1). It is simply wrong to think that James's metaphor about "dead faith" can have only one meaning, i.e., a soteriological one. To claim this is to beg the question.

So, when faith is described as *dead* in James 2, this can easily be understood in context as meaning that (for the purpose being considered) faith is *sterile, ineffectual,* or *unproductive.* Though differing from us theologically, Nicol (*Neotestamentica:* 16) correctly says that the word dead "refers, not to the quality of faith, but to its effect." In addition, Plummer (*General Epistles*, p. 137) has aptly stated: "But St. James nowhere throws doubt on the truth of the unprofitable believer's professions, or on the possibility of believing much and doing nothing." Dibelius (*James*, p. 178) is also right to say: "But in all of the instances [in James] which have been examined thusfar [sic] what is involved is the faith which the Christian has, never the faith of the sinner which first brings him to God . . . The faith which is mentioned in this section can be presupposed in every Christian . . . [James's] intention is not dogmatically oriented, but practically oriented: *he wishes to admonish the Christians to practice their faith, i.e., their Christianity, by works*" (italics his). As far as it goes a better statement cannot be found in the literature on James.

¹⁸ But someone will say, "You have faith, and I have works." Show me your faith without your works, and I will show you my faith by my works. ¹⁹ You believe that there is one God. You do well. Even the demons believe—and tremble!

But James does not expect that his words will go unchallenged among his readers. Even in Christians, the impulse to excuse or cover our failures is strong. So James anticipates his readers' excuse by introducing the words of an imaginary objector. Such alleged objectors were a common stock-in-trade for writers on morals in James's day. The inspired author here employs this well-known literary foil. The entirety of vv 18-19 belong to this hypothetical speaker.

The exact extent and meaning of the objector's words have long been a problem to commentators. The NKJV follows a common understanding in its punctuation of vv 18-19. The words, *You have faith and I have works*, are enclosed in quotation marks by NKJV and this signals that these words alone are taken as the words of an objector. (What they are an objection to has puzzled the commentators.) The remaining words of v 18 and those of v 19 are taken by NKJV as the reply of James, though it is by no means clear how they answer the words attributed to the objector. But *all* punctuation in our English Bibles is the work of editors, since the original manuscript of James would probably have had little or none. We wish to maintain that the text is only correctly understood when the entirety of vv 18-19 (starting with, *You have faith*) is assigned to the objector and *none of it* assigned to James.

In vv 18-19, the specific literary format James uses was familiar from the Greek diatribe, which was a learned and argumentative form of discourse. It has recently been reaffirmed that "James 2:14-26 is particularly diatribal" (Watson, *NTS*: 119). The form employed in 2:18-20 might be called the "objection/reply format." Words such as James's *But someone will say* (v 18) are used to introduce the objection and, when the objection has been stated, a sharp rejoinder is begun with words like James's *But do you want to know, O foolish man* (v 20). As Davids (*Commentary*, p. 126) notes: "*The address 'O foolish person' is part of the strong, direct style of the diatribe* (. . . cf. Hermas *Vis[ions]* 3.8.9; Epict[etus] 2.16.31-32)." Precisely the format we are discussing in James occurs also in Paul at Rom 9:19-20 and in 1 Cor 15:35-36. Note as well in 4 Maccabees 2:24-3:1, the objection: "How is it then, one might say, that . . ." and the reply: "This notion is entirely ridiculous . . ." (RSV). The view of many writers that James's reply has to begin at v 18b ignores the manifest structural signals of James's text, and these writers have failed to produce any comparable text in the relevant literature. This writer regards it as certain that the objector's words extend to the end of v 19.[4]

But what does the objection mean? Since most Greek manuscripts read the word "by" (*ek*) in place of the familiar word "without" (*chōris*) in v 18, we prefer the reading "by" here. (For the textual problem, see Hodges, *BibSac*: 341-50.) The objector's statement may then be given as follows, retaining the Greek word order more exactly than does the NKJV:

> But someone will say:
> "You have faith and I have works. Show me your faith from [*ek*] your works, and I will show you, from [*ek*] my works, my faith. You believe that there is one God; you do well. The demons also believe, and tremble" (2:18-19, author's translation).

The argument which these words express appears to be a *reductio ad absurdum* (reducing someone's claims to absurdity). It is heavy with irony. "It is absurd," says the objector, "to see a close connection between faith and works. For the sake of argument, let's say *you* have faith and *I* have works. Let's start there. *You* can no more start with what you believe and show it to me in your works, than *I* can start with my works and demonstrate what it is that I believe." The objector is confident that both tasks are impossible.[5] The impossibility of showing one's faith from one's works is now demonstrated (so the objector thinks) by this illustration: "Men and demons both believe the same truth (that there is one God), but their faith does not produce the same response. Although this article of faith may move a *human being* to 'do well,' it never moves the *demons* to 'do well.'[6] All *they* can do is tremble. Faith and works, therefore, have no built-in connection at all. The same creed may produce entirely different kinds of conduct. Faith cannot be made visible in works!" With this supposedly unanswerable claim, the objector is made to rest his case.

No doubt James and his readers had heard this argument before. It was precisely the kind of defensive approach people might take when their orthodoxy was not supported by good deeds. They might say, "Faith and works are not really related to each other in the way you say they are, James. So don't criticize the vitality of my faith because I don't do such and such a thing."

20 But do you want to know, O foolish man, that faith without works is dead?

James's reply to the objector's words may be paraphrased: "What a senseless argument! How foolish you are to make it! I still say that without works your faith is dead. Would you like to know why?" Verses 21-23 are James's direct rebuttal of the objection. This is made clear in the Greek text by the singular form of "do you see" (*blepeis*) in v 22. This shows he is addressing the objector. Only with the *you see* (*horate*) of v 24 does James return to the plural and to his readers as a whole.

21 Was not Abraham our father justified by works when he offered Isaac his son on the altar?

In refuting the objection he has cited, James selects the most prestigious name in Jewish history, the patriarch Abraham. He selects also his most honored act of obedience to God, the offering of his own son Isaac. Since in Christian circles it was well known that Abraham was justified *by faith*, James now adds a highly original touch. He was also justified by works! If James's subject matter is kept clearly in mind, we will not fall into the trap of pitting him against the apostle Paul. In no way does James wish to deny that Abraham, or anyone else, could be justified by faith alone. He merely wishes to insist that there is also *another* justification, and it is *by works.*

Of course, there is no such thing as a single justification by faith *plus* works. Nothing James says here suggests that idea. Rather, there are *two kinds* of justification (see v 24). Somewhat surprisingly, to most people, the apostle Paul agrees with this. Writing at what was no doubt a later time than James, Paul states in Rom 4:2, *For if Abraham was justified by works, he has something of which to boast, but not before God.* The form of this statement in Greek does not deny the truth of the point under consideration. The phrase, *but not before God,* strongly suggests that Paul can conceive of a sense in which people *are* justified by works. But, he insists, that is not the way people are justified *before God.* That is, it does not establish their legal standing before Him.

²² Do you see that faith was working together with his works, and by works faith was made perfect?

Therefore, in responding to the kind of person who tried to divorce faith from works in Christian experience, James takes a skillful approach. We may paraphrase it this way: "Wait a minute, you foolish man! You make much of justification by faith, but can't you see how Abraham was *also* justified by works when he offered his son Isaac to God? [v 21]. Isn't it obvious how his faith was cooperating with his works and, in fact, by works his faith was made mature? [v 22]. In this way, too, the full significance of the Scripture about his justification by faith was brought to light, for now he could be called the friend of God" (v 23).

It should be carefully noted that in referring to Abraham's offering of his son Isaac, James has returned to the theme of trials, which is the basic concern of his epistle (see 1:2-18). In Jewish tradition, this story about Abraham represented the supreme trial of the patriarch, over which he had triumphed gloriously. But equally, when James turns to Rahab in v 25, he is likewise dealing with a woman who had triumphed under severe trial. The two stories, standing at the end of a major unit (1:21-2:26), form an implicit *inclusio* (a reference back) carrying the reader's mind back to the point at which the unit on true hearing had begun. The exhortation of 1:21 had sprung from the preceding discussion on Christian trials.

The content of vv 22-23 is rich indeed. It is a pity that it has been so widely misunderstood. The faith which justifies—James never denies that it *does* justify!—can have an active and vital role in the life of the obedient believer. As with Abraham, it can be the dynamic for great acts of obedience. In the process, faith itself can be *made perfect*, i.e., "perfected" (*eteleiōthē*). The Greek word suggests development and maturation. Faith is thus nourished and strengthened by works.

It would hardly be possible to find a better illustration of James's point anywhere in the Bible. The faith by which Abraham was justified was directed toward God's promise about his seed (Gen 15:4-6), a promise that reaffirmed the initial promise of Gen 12:1-3, which carried soteriological significance (see Gal 3:6-9). But Abraham's faith was also implicitly faith in a God of resurrection. Referring to the occasion of Gen 15:6, Paul wrote:

> And not being weak in faith, he did not consider his own body, already dead (since he was about a hundred years old), and the deadness of Sarah's womb. He did not waver at the promise of God through unbelief, but was strengthened in faith, giving glory to God, and being fully convinced that what He had promised He was also able to perform (Rom 4:19-21).

Abraham had confidence that the God in whom he believed could overcome the deadness of his own body and of Sarah's womb. But it was only through the testing with Isaac that this implicit faith in God's resurrection power becomes a specific conviction that God could literally raise a person physically from the dead to fulfill His oath. Accordingly, the author of Hebrews declares:

> By faith Abraham, when he was tested, offered up his only begotten

son, of whom it was said, "In Isaac your seed shall be called,"
concluding that God was able to raise him up, even from the dead, from
which he also received him in a figurative sense" (Heb 11:17-19).

Thus the faith of Abraham was strengthened and matured by works! From a conviction that God could overcome a "deadness" in his own body (inability to beget children), he moved to the assurance that God could actually resurrect his son's body from literal, physical death. In the process of carrying out the divine command to sacrifice his beloved boy, his faith grew and reached new heights of confidence in God.

23 And the Scripture was fulfilled which says, "Abraham believed God, and it was accounted to him for righteousness." And he was called the friend of God.

In this way, too, the Scripture that spoke of his original justification was fulfilled. That statement (Gen 15:6) was not a prophecy, of course. But its implications were richly developed and exposed by the subsequent record of Abraham's obedience.[7] Abraham's works filled this ancient text full of meaning, so to speak, by showing the extent to which the faith of Gen 15:6 could develop and undergird a life of obedience. Simple and uncomplicated though it was at first, Abraham's justifying faith had potential ramifications which only his works, built on it, could disclose.

A case can be made (see Jacobs, *NTS*: 457-64) that the story about Abraham offering Isaac had already been connected with Gen 15:6 in Jewish exegesis before James's time. For example, the author of 1 Maccabees 2:52 wrote: "Was not Abraham found faithful when tested, and it was reckoned to him as righteousness?" The author was apparently tying together Gen 15 and 22 so that Gen 15:6 becomes a proleptic statement about the grounds on which Abraham was awarded righteousness. But this works-righteousness view of Gen 15:6 is not at all the view of Paul or James. That James understood the text as referring to justification by faith is clear from his reference to this kind of justification in the very next verse (v 24). But James does not adopt the legalistic interpretation of Gen 15:6. Instead, James sees Gen 15:6 as ascribing to Abraham just that sort of faith which would be required in order for Abraham later to obey God and offer Him his son. In that sense Gen 15:6 was pregnant with implications about what could take place in the future if Abraham was willing to *act* on the basis of the faith that had justified him. When Abraham *did* act on his faith, that faith was made fruitful in his superb obedience to God concerning Isaac. When his justifying faith was *put to work*, the implications of his original faith were wonderfully realized and Gen 15:6 was in that way "fulfilled."

And now he could be called *the friend of God,* not only by God Himself, but also by men (cf. Isa 41:8; 2 Chr 20:7). This is in fact the name by which Abraham has been known down through the centuries in many lands and by at least three religions (Judaism, Christianity, and Islam). Had Abraham not obeyed God in the greatest test of his life, he would still have been justified by the faith he exercised in Gen 15:6. But by allowing that faith to be *alive* in his *works*, he attained an enviable title among countless millions of people. In this way he was also justified by works (before men; cf. Rom 4:2).

When a person is justified by faith, he or she finds an unqualified acceptance before God. As Paul puts it, such an individual is one *to whom God imputes righteousness without works* (Rom 4:6). But only God can see this spiritual transaction. When, however, one is justified by works he or she achieves an intimacy with God that is *manifest to others*. He or she can then be called a "friend of God," even as Jesus said, *"You are My friends if you do whatever I command you"* (John 15:14; see also the discussion of Jas 4:4).

²⁴ You see then that a man is justified by works, and not by faith only.

Leaving the imagined objector behind, James returns in vv 24-26 to address his readers directly. (See comment on v 20.) His statement here confirms what we observed above (v 21), that there are *two kinds* of justification, not one kind conditioned on faith *plus* works. James's words do *not* mean a man is justified by works, and not [*justified*] by faith only [or, *alone*]. Instead, James's words should be read like this: "You see then that a man is justified by works, and not only [justified] by faith." The key to this understanding is the Greek adverb "only" (*monon*), which does not qualify (i.e., modify) the word *faith*, since the form would then have been *monēs*. As an adverb, however, it modifies the verb *justified* implied in the second clause. James is saying that a by-faith justification is not the *only* kind of justification there is. There is also a by-works justification. The former type is *before God*; the latter type is *before men*.[8]

25 Likewise, was not Rahab the harlot also justified by works when she received the messengers and sent them out another way?

This is precisely what is now illustrated in the additional case of Rahab. James does *not* say, "Was not Rahab the harlot justified by faith *and* works?" James knows of no such justification. Rather, Rahab, like Abraham before her, *was justified by works* in front of other people——i.e., before the nation of Israel among whom she came to live. (For Rahab's honored role in Jewish thought, see Laws, *Epistle*, p. 137.)

Rahab, however, is superbly suited to tie James's thoughts together. The passage had begun, as we have seen, with a reference to his theme of "saving the life" (v 14; 1:21). Not surprisingly, Rahab is selected as a striking example of a person whose physical life was "saved" precisely because she had works. With James's words the statement of the writer of Hebrews can be profitably compared. In 11:31, that author writes of her:

> By faith the harlot Rahab did not perish with those who did not believe, when she had received the spies with peace.

Notice that the author of Hebrews points to her faith and lays the stress on the fact that she *received* the spies. James, by contrast, points to the fact that *she sent them out another way.*

Why does James do this? The answer has considerable significance for James's argument.

Although Rahab's *faith* began to operate the moment she *received the messengers,* she could not really be *justified by works* until she had *sent them out another way.* This is obvious when the story in Joshua 2 is carefully considered. Up until the last minute, she could still have betrayed the spies. Had she so desired, she could have sent their pursuers after them. That the spies had lingering doubts about her loyalty is suggested by their words in Josh 2:20, *"And if you tell this business of ours, then we will be free from your oath."* But the successful escape of the spies demonstrated that Rahab was truly a *friend of God* because she was also *their* friend. In this way, *Rahab* was *justified by works.*

And in the process, she saved her own life and her family's! Her faith, therefore, was very much *alive* because it was an active, working faith. Though she was a prostitute—and both inspired writers remind us that she was—her living faith triumphed over the natural consequences of her sin. While all the rest of the inhabitants of Jericho perished under the divine judgment which Israel executed, *she lived* because her *faith lived!*

²⁶ For as the body without the spirit is dead, so faith without works is dead also.

James therefore wishes his readers to know that works are in fact the vitalizing "spirit" which keeps one's faith alive, in the same way that the human spirit keeps the human body alive. Whenever a Christian ceases to act on his faith, that faith atrophies and becomes little more than a creedal corpse. "Dead orthodoxy" is a danger that has always confronted Christian people, and we do well to take heed to this danger. But the antidote is a simple one: Faith remains vital and alive as long as it is being translated into real works of living obedience.⁹

ENDNOTES

[1] For a fuller discussion of the subject of inheriting God's kingdom, see my chapter entitled, "Who Are the Heirs?" in *The Gospel Under Siege*, 2d ed. (Dallas, Redención Viva, 1992), pp. 127-41.

[2] Some writers *do* admit this. For example, Lorenzen writes: "The original Greek makes it clear . . . that the rhetorical question calls for a negative answer: No! Faith without works cannot save! Works are necessary for salvation." See ET: 231. Cf. also Nicol in *Neotestamentica*, p. 22, where he states that, "logically . . . good works must be a condition for justification," and that "Paul might say: you must do good works, otherwise in the end God will not justify you."

[3] Even Robertson, *Epistle*, p. 94, n. 2, assigns to the article "almost the original demonstrative force." But this is *extremely* unlikely here when it is not even true later in the passage where the article appears with faith at 2:17, 20, 22 (twice), and 26. Any student of the original language can examine James's text and see for himself that the article occurs with faith only when faith is a subject or has a possessive word qualifying it (as in verse 18). Otherwise there is no article. There is no subtle significance to the article in 2:14. Quite rightly Dibelius rejects the special stress on the article: "Here Jas uses the article before faith . . . but this is not to be read 'this faith', as many interpreters from Bede to Mayor have argued. Jas is not speaking of any particular brand of faith . . . The only attributive which is expressed . . . is this: faith which 'has' no works. But this is still the Christian faith and not an 'alleged, false faith.'" So much for building theology on an undetectable grammatical nuance! See Dibelius, *James*, p. 152.

[4] The evident unity of vv 18-19 as constituting the words of a single speaker is strongly attested in the literature on this passage. Many of those who have accepted this unity, however, have regarded the speaker not as an objector but as a pious ally who takes James's point of view. But this explanation is rightly dismissed by Davids *(James*, p. 124) because "no one has yet been able to find a case where this common stylistic introduction did not introduce an opposing or disagreeing voice." Among those treating the two verses as a unity are: Johnstone, *Lectures*, pp. 188-90; Dale, *Epistle*, pp. 70-71; Knowling (apparently), *Epistle*, pp. 56-59; Mayor, *Epistle*, p. 101; Donker, ZNW: 227-40; Vouga, *L'Épître*, p. 87; Martin (hesitantly), *James*, pp. 86-90.

[5] The use of the challenge to "show me" in an ironical sense is well documented by Dibelius, *James*, pp. 154-55, n. 29. Especially parallel to James is a passage from *Ad Autolycus* 1.2, in which the apologist Theophilus writes: "But even if you should say, 'Show me your God', I too might say to you, 'Show me your Man and I also will show you my God.'" But this same ironic and unfulfillable demand is frequent in Epictetus, for example in the

biting scorn of *Discourses* 3.22.99: "Who in the world are you? The bull of the herd or the queen of the beehive? Show me the symbols of your rulership!" For additional examples see Dibelius.

[6] The Greek phrase *kalōs poieis* (*you do well*) is taken by us in the sense of "do good," "do right," which seems the most appropriate sense in Matt 5:44; 12:12; Luke 6:27. It is also viable in Acts 10:33 ("you did the right thing to come") and even in James 2:8 ("If you keep the royal law . . . you are doing what's right"). Attention should be given also to the secular examples cited by Mayor, *Epistle*, p. 101. In Hellenistic Greek one would be unwise to insist pedantically on the good/well differentiation so dear to strict English grammarians!

[7] Hort (*Epistle*, p. 64) explains *the Scripture was fulfilled* (v 23) as follows: "The Divine word spoken is conceived of as receiving a completion so to speak in acts or events which are done or come to pass in accordance with it. The idea of filling, or giving fullness to, is always contained in the biblical use of fulfilling, though not always in the same sense."

[8] Worthy of note is Darby's comment on this passage: "James, remark, never says that works justify us *before God* [italics his]; for God can see the faith without its works. He knows that life is there. It is in exercise with regard to Him, towards Him, by trust in His word, in Himself, by receiving His testimony in spite of everything within and without. This God sees and knows. But when our fellow creatures are in question, when it must be said 'shew,' then faith, life, shows itself in works." Darby, *Synopsis*, 5:271.

[9] A word should be said about John Calvin's own treatment of James 2:14-26. To the surprise of some, perhaps, we do not find in Calvin anything that reflects the theological tangle into which Reformed theology has fallen. In two critical points, Calvin agrees with the present writer *against* modern Reformed theology. The two points are these: (1) justification by works does not refer to our justification before God, but rather before men; (2) our good works are not the basis of our assurance of salvation.

Calvin says these things plainly: "So when the sophists set James against Paul, they are deceived by the double meaning of the term 'justification'. When Paul says we are justified by faith, he means precisely that we have won a verdict of righteousness in the sight of God. James has quite another intention, that the man who professes himself to be faithful *should demonstrate the truth of his fidelity by works*. James did not mean to teach us *where the confidence of our salvation should rest*—which is the very point on which Paul does insist. So let us avoid the false reasoning which has trapped the sophists, by taking note of the double meaning: To Paul, the word denotes our free imputation of righteousness before the judgment seat of God; to James, *the demonstration of righteousness from its effects, before men*; which we may deduce from the preceding words, *Shew me thy faith, etc.* [italics in the text]. In the latter sense, we may admit without controversy that man is justified by works, just as you might say a man is enriched by the purchase of a large and costly estate, since his wealth, which beforehand he kept out of sight in a strongbox, has become well-known" (italics added except in the case specified). Calvin, *Comm.* James 2.21.

Neither does Calvin fall here into the hopeless quagmire of talking about a "spurious" faith which simulates the real thing so that true faith can only be recognized by works. Calvin will not give the name of faith to those whom he considers James to be attacking. He writes, for example: "He [James] is speaking of false profession, and his words make this certain. He does not start, 'If a man has faith', but 'If a man says he has faith . . .' Plainly he implies that there are hypocrites who make an *empty boast* of the word, when they have no real claim on it." A few sentences later he says, "Just remember, he is not speaking out of his own understanding of the word when he calls it 'faith', but is *disputing with those who pretend insincerely to faith, but are entirely without it*" (on 2:14; italics added).

Although I might quarrel with Calvin's exegesis here, at least he is consistent with the fundamental premises of his own theology. Since, for Calvin, assurance was of the essence of saving faith, he does not ascribe this "false profession" to any who have found that assurance, but describes those without works as *insincere* pretenders who make a *false* claim to faith. Thus he will also ascribe to such people only "an indifferent and formal understanding of God" (commenting on 2:14) or "a certain uninformed opinion of God" (on 2:19) or "a bare and empty awareness of God" (on 2:23). This is a far cry from his own definition of faith as "a steady and certain knowledge of the divine benevolence toward us" which is "founded on the truth of the gratuitous promise in Christ" (*Institutes* III.ii.7). Calvin does *not* hold that faith must be subjectively verified *to ourselves* by works, but objectively verified *before men*.

CHAPTER 4

Be Slow to Speak

(James 3:1-18)

B. By Being Slow to Speak (3:1-18)

1. Because the tongue is a dangerous instrument for
   displaying wisdom (3:1-12)

With 2:26 James has concluded his discussion about being
swift to hear (1:21-2:26). He has demonstrated that proper
hearing involves *works*, by which he means especially works of
compassion and love to the poor and needy. Without such
works, a man's faith loses its vitality and life and becomes a
mere "dead orthodoxy." But in the absence of *works*, there is
usually an abundance of *words*. Those whose faith is not being
translated into deeds are very likely to be eager to *talk* about
their faith and to instruct others in its delicate theological
nuances! Such is human nature. So it is fully logical that James
should now begin a discussion which relates to the second
command of 1:19-20 (see the comments there), namely, *be
slow to speak*. The result of this discussion is nothing less than
the most famous passage on the tongue in all of literature.
Here, in fact, we have the Holy Spirit's candid assessment of
a fault most of us have: talking too much!

**¹My brethren, let not many of you become teachers, knowing
that we shall receive a stricter judgment.**

In the early Church, the gatherings of believers were less
formal than the morning worship service familiar to so many
today. We may conclude from 1 Corinthians 11-14 that the
meetings were largely unstructured (except for the Lord's
Supper) and were open to any of the men who wished to make

an oral contribution (the women, however, were silent: 1 Cor 14:34-35). In such a context, any brother might rise to give the church instruction, whether or not he was particularly suited, or gifted, for this task. James begins his discussion of the tongue by addressing this tendency. He believes that *not many of you* should *become teachers*. The reason? Very simply, the man who used his tongue to teach would be held to a higher standard, *a stricter judgment*, at the Judgment Seat of Christ, than someone who had not so used his tongue. It is noteworthy that James includes himself among those who teach: *we shall receive a stricter judgment*. It was a solemn responsibility to assume the role of a teacher in the Christian Church. James thinks most of his readers will be better off to avoid this role.

² For we all stumble in many things. If anyone does not stumble in word, he is a perfect man, able also to bridle the whole body.

After all, James states, *we all stumble in many things* (once again the *we* includes James himself). But if this is true in a general way, it is even more true of the tongue. Indeed, if it were possible to avoid stumbling in the use of the tongue, it would be possible to avoid *all* stumbling. Such a person would be *a perfect man*. The Greek word for *perfect* is *teleios*, which does not mean specifically "sinless," but probably here means something like "flawless"—i.e., "a man without a flaw." But as the rest of the chapter makes plain, no such man exists, since *no man can tame the tongue* (v 8).

³ Indeed, we put bits in horses' mouths that they may obey us, and we turn their whole body. ⁴ Look also at ships: although they are so large and are driven by fierce winds, they are turned by a very small rudder wherever the pilot desires.

James now goes on to emphasize the capabilities of this small member of the human body. It is true that bridling the tongue means one can also control his *whole body* (v 2), and this should not be surprising. In the same way, *we put bits in horses' mouths* and are able thereby to control the horse's *whole body*. Moreover, sizable *ships* are controlled even in *fierce winds* by a relatively tiny attachment: *a very small rudder*. Thus a great ship, like a horse, is subject to human control and is *turned . . . wherever the pilot desires* by a very small instrument. Thus far, James has stressed only the tongue's potential as a tiny "bit" or *rudder* capable of controlling man's "whole body" (v 2). That is to say, human beings can control their own actions provided they first can control the *rudder*— namely, the human tongue. To a large extent our actions are determined by the things we say.

To use a simple illustration: if we say, "I'll come over tonight," we are far more likely to go than if we say nothing about whether we will or won't. Even if we do *not* go, after saying that we will, we are easily drawn into making excuses which are deceptive. These excuses may require further actions or additional lies, and so on. This principle can be extended into every facet of our lives.

⁵ Even so the tongue is a little member and boasts great things. See how great a forest a little fire kindles!

In view of the tongue's potential as a "controller" of behavior, this *little member* of our body can boast of great exploits, i.e., it *boasts great things*. The Greek word translated by this last phrase is *megalauchei* (according to the great majority of manuscripts) and carries negative overtones of proud bragging. No doubt the choice of this word here is deliberate on James's part. This verse, for him, is actually a transition statement which moves from considering the tongue's *potential* (vv 3-4) to considering its *potential dangers* (vv 5b-6). It is almost as if, when the tongue "speaks" of its great exploits, it cannot refrain from "boasting" about them. All of us will recognize this trait in ourselves, for who indeed can speak of his accomplishments without pride or boasting?

The transition to a negative assessment of the tongue begins, therefore, with the expression *boasts great things* and moves swiftly on to compare the tongue to *a little fire* (we might

say: a 'spark' or a 'match') which results in a raging inferno in
a *great . . . forest*. How often some casual remark has touched
off a firestorm of trouble in human experience! It has hap-
pened at every level of human life.

**⁶And the tongue is a fire, a world of iniquity. The tongue is so
set among our members that it defiles the whole body, and
sets on fire the course of nature; and it is set on fire by hell.**

Therefore it can be truly said that *the tongue is a fire* or,
perhaps better, "the tongue is *fire*" (as we could also translate). To play loosely with the tongue is to play dangerously
with *fire*. Why? Because the tongue is also *a world of iniquity*
(similarly, RSV, JB, NIV). The Greek phrase here *(ho kosmos tēs
adikias)*, which might also be rendered "an iniquitous world,"
suggests that a veritable cosmos of evil lies present within the
tiny confines of this dangerous member of our body. There is
no kind of evil at all which cannot be ignited in human life by
this tiny firetrap! Nothing that is wicked in the external world
lies beyond the range of "the world of evil" which is internal
to the human tongue itself.

That is how the tongue functions among the members of our
body. In the words, *the tongue is so set,* we probably have a
reference back to the first part of this verse. The KJV and NKJV,
however, take them as a reference *forward* to what follows and
introduce the word *that* into the text. But there is nothing in
the Greek to correspond to the word *that* and the remaining
statements seem clearly to be qualifying statements about *the
tongue*. It would be preferable to translate: "That is how,
among our members, the tongue is set, which defiles the
whole body . . ." The word for *set* is *kathistēmi*, which is of
flexible character in Greek usage, and here probably means
something like "plays its role." James means that the tongue
plays the role of a dangerous fire and of a "world of wickedness" (see first part of this verse).

No wonder then that the role of the tongue makes it a
physical member *which defiles the whole body, and sets on fire the
course of nature* (better, "the course of life": Davids, *Commen-*

tary, p. 143). By the words which we speak we may come to feel completely filthy; furthermore, our words can lead us to physical acts that defile the entire physical self, as is the case with sins like adultery and fornication. Moreover, our words can lead not only to overall defilement, but they can also inflame the entire course of our lives by the ongoing consequences which they produce.

The phrase found in this verse, *the course of nature (ton trochon tēs geneseōs)*, is a difficult one but is perhaps best understood in the sense of "the course (or, cycle) of existence." The Greek word for *course (trochos)* is literally "wheel," so that the phrase suggests a metaphor. Tasker's comments *(Epistle*, p. 76) are clarifying:

> The wheel, because its function is to revolve and because it is a circle always revolving on the same axis, was a common symbol among the ancients both for the changeableness and the completed 'round' of human life. Each human life rolls onward, as it were, from birth to death through many phases and changes, in order to complete its allotted 'cycle.'

(For the wide currency of this concept in James's day, see Laws, *Epistle*, pp. 150-51.)

Someone has compared James's imagery here to the wheel of a fast-moving chariot whose axle is on fire. The tongue, says James, can set fire to the ongoing "wheel" of our experience so that our lives roll forward heated and endangered by things our tongues may have said. But the fire that ignites our *course* of life is itself often ignited *by hell (tēs Geennēs)*. Thus the metaphor of the wheel is concluded by another metaphor in which "hell" is an obvious metonymy for Satan himself (see Mitton, *Epistle*, p. 129). That Satan can and does inspire evil words is clearly illustrated in Scripture (e.g., Job 2:4, 9; see Matt 16:22-23 where Peter spoke words inspired by Satan). Thus James warns us of the ongoing consequences of our wrong words which, in turn, are often put on our lips by Satan himself.

⁷For every kind of beast and bird, of reptile and creature of the sea, is tamed and has been tamed by mankind. ⁸But no man can tame the tongue. It is an unruly evil, full of deadly poison.

After the grim portrayal of the tongue's capacity for harm in v 6, we would like to feel that so dangerous an instrument can be kept fully under control. Unfortunately this is not the case. For although human beings have had success in training virtually *every kind of beast and bird, of reptile and creature of the sea*, no one can claim a similar success with the tongue, since *no man can tame the tongue*. Even the greatest of God's servants—our Lord excepted—have failed to completely control their tongues. In fact, Moses, one of the greatest of all, was excluded from the Promised Land because *he spoke rashly with his lips* (Ps 106:33).

Precisely, then, because it cannot be finally tamed while we are in our earthly bodies, the tongue remains *an unruly evil, full of deadly poison*. The Christian needs to remember at all times that he carries in his mouth what could be compared to a poisonous viper, and that serpentine instrument can affect others in a way that even results in their death (for example, ridicule of a suicidal person). Since the Christian can never relax with the assumption that this "viper" is fully under control, he or she must be especially alert against its most disastrous eruptions.

⁹With it we bless our God and Father, and with it we curse men, who have been made in the similitude of God. ¹⁰Out of the same mouth proceed blessing and cursing. My brethren, these things ought not to be so.

He must be alert as well to its horrifying inconsistencies. The same lips that *bless our God and Father*, in a hymn or prayer of praise, may also *curse* and vilify *men* (even our Christian brothers) despite the fact that they bear *the similitude of God* who created them in His image (Gen 1:26-27). (The Bible does not teach that the image of God has been *obliterated* in fallen man, however much it has been *defaced* by sin.) Thus, *the same mouth* can become the source of *blessing and cursing*—sometimes in such a swift transition that mere seconds suffice to move from one of these modes of speech to the other. In a deliberately understated assertion, James informs his Christian *brethren* that *these things ought not to be so*. But true as that is, they *will* be so to some extent in each of us, and our task is to find the help of God to make them less and less so as we grow in Christ.

¹¹ Does a spring send forth fresh water and bitter from the same opening?

Furthermore, such behavior by the tongue is unsuitable (it *ought not to be*) because it flies in the face of the consistency and predictability of so much in nature around us. For example, *a spring* does not inconsistently *send forth fresh water and bitter*. For the word rendered *send forth*, James uses the Greek verb *bryei* which means "to pour or gush forth." The analogy seems to imply delicately the way our mouths pour out words, often so disharmonious and inconsistent with one another that it is almost like yielding bitter and sweet water at the same time.

¹² Can a fig tree, my brethren, bear olives, or a grapevine bear figs? Thus no spring yields both salt water and fresh.

In addition, the tongue is not only inconsistent (v 11), but it also behaves contrary to natural expectation. On *a fig tree* one does not reasonably expect to find *olives*, nor does one look for *figs* on *a grapevine*. No more should one expect lips that were designed to bless *our God and Father* (v 9) to produce vilification of humans who are *made in the similitude of God* (v 9). Yet, too often, this anomaly meets us even in Christians.

James now concludes his warnings against the untamable tongue by a renewed reference to a *spring*. But this closing statement is somewhat different from the one just made in v 11. Those who lived in the arid conditions of the Middle East knew the value of a good spring of water. James's reference to fresh and bitter water was largely a reference to the *taste* of the water. One either enjoyed the spring's water or he did not, though he might drink it anyway in an emergency. But *salt water and fresh* water were qualitatively distinct, and men and animals could live on the latter kind of water but not on the former. Not only does the tongue (unlike any natural spring) produce both pleasant and unpleasant words ("fresh" and "bitter"), but it produces words that can destroy (*salt water*) and words that can sustain life (*fresh* water). If his readers used their tongues too much, they could readily expect both negative and positive results of a far-reaching character. The writer of Proverbs (18:21) expressed the thought well: *Death and life are in the power of the tongue, and those who love it* [the tongue] *will eat its fruit* [death and life].

2. Because holy conduct is the safe instrument for displaying wisdom (3:13-18)

The tongue, then, was not a wise thing for James's readers to use very much. For that reason, they should be reluctant to try to become teachers in their local congregations (see v 1). If they thought they had wisdom to share with their fellow Christians, it would be better to find another way to do that than by the use of their tongues. The dangers and deficiencies of the tongue (vv 6b-12) obviously implied the ancient truth: *In the multitude of words sin is not lacking, but he who restrains his lips is wise* (Prov 10:19). But if that was so, what could James suggest?

13 Who is wise and understanding among you? Let him show by good conduct that his works are done in the meekness of wisdom.

James's suggestion is clear and specific. Was anyone among them *wise and understanding*? The way to demonstrate this fact was *by good conduct*. Naturally such *conduct* would be characterized by *works*, as James has already shown (1:21—2:26). The NKJV, however, slightly distorts the text by introducing an italicized *that* which is unnecessary. We do better to translate: "Let him show [display] his works through good conduct with the meekness of [derived from] wisdom." Instead of boldly (and arrogantly!) verbalizing the wisdom they thought they possessed, James's readers are challenged to demonstrate it by their lifestyle in that gentle spirit (*praütēs: meekness*) which was always a mark of true wisdom. See our Lord's declaration that if He teaches us, we will learn to be gentle (*praos*) (Matt 11:29).

¹⁴ But if you have bitter envy and self-seeking in your hearts, do not boast and lie against the truth.

But *meekness* was sorely lacking, it appears, in some of the Christian churches James was addressing (see 4:1-2). James therefore warns them that *if* they had *bitter envy and self-seeking* in their *hearts*, any effort to display God's wisdom could be called lying *against the truth.* How dare they rise in the Christian assembly, ostensibly to impart God's wisdom to their Christian brothers, while at the same time they were actually motivated by *envy* of other Christians and by a spirit of rivalry! The word translated *self-seeking (eritheia)*, though rare before NT times, probably connotes the kind of egotism that is expressed by an ambition to get ahead of others. The situation James has in mind has been repeated numberless times in Christian churches. Christians who wish a higher status in the church than someone else, of whom they are envious, often seek some prominent role which will satisfy this fleshly ambition. They may even delude themselves in imagining they are serving God. In the unstructured meetings of the early Church (see discussion on v 1), the easiest way to rise above others was to be perceived as a preeminently wise and understanding teacher of the church. But this kind of mentality is censured severely here by James.

To behave in the way James is describing was to *boast and lie against the truth.* The Greek verb for *boast, katakauchasthe,* is the same word used in 2:13 about mercy triumphing over judgment. The probable meaning here is similar. A man who dares wield the truth of God as an instrument to satisfy his own *envy and self-seeking,* as he professes to teach that truth, is guilty of "triumphing over" the truth. That is, he arrogantly tramples down the truth as if it were a thing subordinate to his own personal ambitions. He seeks to use God's truth for his own selfish ends, rather than to minister it for the good of others. Such conduct is also a lie *against the truth*, since this conduct only pretends to be in submission to the truth. In fact, such behavior is in itself contrary to the truth one is professing to teach.

¹⁵ This wisdom does not descend from above, but is earthly, sensual, demonic.

If that is the way the would-be teacher was trying to show his wisdom (see v 13), he was misguided. He was showing a kind of *wisdom* all right, but it was not the kind he thought. *This wisdom*, says James, is not of heavenly origin. Instead it is *earthly, sensual, demonic*. This withering indictment was just what such behavior deserved. The "wisdom" of the self-promoting teacher was precisely the kind found among unsaved men who shrewdly plotted their own advancement. Thus it was *earthly*. Then, too, it was totally unspiritual and the mere product of human desire. Thus it was *sensual* (*psychikos*: "soulish"). Finally, since it was inspired and encouraged by the spirits which served Satan, it was *demonic*, with all the spiritual damage implied by that tragic fact.

¹⁶ For where envy and self-seeking exist, confusion and every evil thing are there.

Basically, wherever *envy and self-seeking* were at work in the Christian Church, there were always two inescapable consequences. One of these was *confusion* (*akatastasia*: "disorder," "unruliness"), and the other was *every evil thing* (*pragma*: "deed," "event"). How often this inspired statement has proved true in churches where individuals seek prominence out of a spirit of jealousy or proud ambition! Characteristically the local church where this occurs is thrown into turmoil, and factionalism and evil things are said and done which have no place in the Christian fellowship. Thus the work of Satan becomes unmistakable.

[17] But the wisdom that is from above is first pure, then peaceable, gentle, willing to yield, full of mercy and good fruits, without partiality and without hypocrisy.

In sharpest contrast with all this stands the true heavenly wisdom: *the wisdom that is from above.* The primary characteristic of such divinely bestowed wisdom is the fact that it is *pure.* It is free of the moral contamination of *envy and self-seeking* (v 16) and is marked by true devotion to God. As a result, it is also *peaceable (eirēnikos)* and is therefore concerned about harmony with, and among, the brethren. But its peace-loving nature also makes such wisdom both *gentle* (or, "kind": *epieikēs*) as well as *willing to yield* (or, "compliant": *eupeithēs*). This kindness and compliancy mean that such wisdom does not rigidly insist on its own way, but is graciously anxious to go out of its way for other believers. The last three qualities (peaceable, kind, compliant) all begin with the Greek letter epsilon *(e)* and they are alliterative when put together as James arranges them here. They also describe traits which tend to appear together in an individual.

But if purity, peaceableness, kindness, and compliancy have pride of place in James's list, it is equally true that heaven-wrought wisdom will be *full of mercy and good fruits, without partiality and without hypocrisy.* The attentive reader will hear echoes in these words of earlier themes in this epistle. *Mercy* recalls our mind to 1:27 and 2:13. *Good fruits* echoes 1:22-25 and 2:14-26, while *without partiality* evokes 2:1-13 (although the Greek word here is different from the one in 2:1).[1] *Without hypocrisy* echoes the near context, specifically v 14. In short, along with the first four qualities, these are the aspects of *good conduct* (v 13) which verify a person's wisdom in a way that words by themselves are powerless to do.

[18] Now the fruit of righteousness is sown in peace by those who make peace.

Such conduct as James has just described is obviously the kind that will promote peace and tranquility in Christian churches, rather than *confusion and every evil thing* (v 16), which are the fruit of *envy and self-seeking*. The person who behaves as v 17 describes is among *those who make peace*. (The translation, *by those who make peace* [*tois poiousin eirēnēn*], takes *poiousin* as a dative of agent [by] rather than of advantage [for]. The dative of agent is found earlier in this chapter in the phrase translated *by mankind* in v 7, and it gives the best sense here.) Thus, as a peacemaker, the one who demonstrates the heavenly wisdom of v 17 is like a sower in a field. His behavior (his seed) has its ultimate *fruit* in *righteousness*, since righteousness among believers grows and flourishes when they dwell together *in peace*. Given James's concern for congregational peace (cf. 4:1-3), it is probable that the phrase *in peace* goes actually with the phrase, *the fruit of righteousness*, rather than with *sown*, as in the NKJV (i.e., we should read: "the fruit of righteousness in peace, is sown by . . ."). The point is that this righteousness is experienced in an atmosphere of peace when the peacemaker has done his work of sowing and the harvest has been reaped in the church.

James would surely agree with the psalmist: *Behold, how good and how pleasant it is for brethren to dwell together in unity!* (Ps 133:1).

ENDNOTES

[1] Here the word is *adiakritos*; there it is *prosōpolēpsia* (lit., "face-acceptance," respect of persons).

CHAPTER 5

Be Slow to Anger

(James 4:1—5:6)

C. By Being Slow to Wrath (4:1—5:6)

1. Since wrath is created by worldliness (4:1-5)

The preceding paragraph (3:13-18) has given us a much clearer view of the churches to which James is writing. Some of them, at least, were in turmoil due to *envy and self-seeking* (3:14), leading to competition among individuals to excel one another as *wise and understanding* teachers in the church (3:1, 13). Not surprisingly, in such an atmosphere there was *confusion and every evil thing* (3:16). We are less than startled, therefore, that such assemblies of Christians were rocked by *wars and fights* (v 1). Since that was the case, James now embarks on an elaboration of the third of his three fundamental commands in 1:19, namely, the command to *be slow to wrath*. As the situation in the churches demonstrated all too well, *the wrath of man does not produce the righteousness of God* (1:20). What it *does* produce are the very conflicts that James now turns to address!

> **¹ Where do wars and fights come from among you? Do they not come from your desires for pleasure that war in your members?**

What then was the cause of the *wars and fights* among his readers? *Where* did they *come from*? The answer is sharp and direct. Such conflicts arise, James states, *from your desires for pleasure*. The NKJV surely has the correct idea here even though no Greek word corresponds to the English words *desires for*. James's statement virtually personifies the word *pleasures* so that these *pleasures* become like hostile soldiers who wage *war* within his readers, i.e., *in your* (physical) *members*.

James's statement is thoroughly Pauline and recalls especially Rom 7:23, *But I see another law in my members, warring against the law of my mind, and bringing me into captivity to the law of sin which is in my members.* Not all pleasure is evil (see 1 Tim 6:17), but James's readers were caught up in the inward competition between good desires and bad desires. Specifically, among other things, the conflict was between the "pleasure" of obeying God's law of liberty (1:25) and the "pleasure" of being honored in the church above others whom one envied. The former "pleasure" led to God's blessing (1:25) and to the preservation of one's life (1:21), and the latter "pleasure" produced turmoil in the church (3:16) and led toward death (1:15).

Why were the Christians at war with *one another*? It was because they experienced *war within themselves*, as good and evil impulses did battle with each other!

² You lust and do not have. You murder and covet and cannot obtain. You fight and war. Yet you do not have because you do not ask.

Their tumultuous inner life is now discussed in terms of its utterly frustrating nature. *You lust and do not have*: what they wanted was out of their reach. *You murder and covet and cannot obtain.* It is unlikely that James means that his readers literally committed murder, but, as the apostle John has declared, *whoever hates his brother is a murderer* (1 John 3:15). Davids (*Commentary*, p. 158) notes that murder "in a metaphorical sense" is connected "to the sins of the tongue and to jealousy in many ancient texts."

In their jealous hostility toward some Christian brother or sister, James's readers were doubtless guilty of "wishing him away" ("I wish he was dead") and then of coveting what they hoped they might *obtain* if he actually *were* dead. But since this murderous spirit could not be actualized (too risky, too shameful, too sinful, etc.), it only accentuated the readers' frustration. Despite their mental murder and intense coveting, they were left where they started. They could not *obtain* what they coveted. All that was left was to continue the brother-versus-brother conflict in all its unpleasant aspects: hence, says James, *you fight and war*. Out of your deep frustration, James is saying, you turn your church into a battlefield.

No doubt some readers will feel shocked that James could speak this way to his Christian brothers, whom he regards as born again (1:18). But this shock betrays an unrealistic attitude toward the faults and failures of Christian people. It reflects also a superficial or legalistic reading of the NT. One needs only to study 1 Corinthians, for example, to learn how numerous and serious are the faults one can encounter in Christian assemblies! Salvation is by grace through faith and absolutely has to be, since even the best among us *fall short of the glory of God* (Rom 3:23). But even when we do not suffer from the exact faults of James's earliest Christian readers, if we examine our own hearts honestly, we will recognize that we have the potential for such faults. If we do *not* recognize that fact, we are probably suffering from one of the gravest faults of all: self-righteousness!

But as tragic as was the selfish inward frustration of his readership, equally bad was the fact that they had not turned to God to meet their needs: *You do not have because you do not ask*.

³You ask and do not receive, because you ask amiss, that you may spend it on your pleasures.

On the other hand they *did ask*, but their requests were wrongly conceived. (The words *you ask amiss* are equivalent to "you ask badly," where "badly" stands for the Greek word *kakōs*.) Their requests were bad precisely because they were selfish. Whatever they were asking God for, they intended to *spend it on* their *pleasures*. The phrase is a remarkable one. By using the word *spend* (*dapanaō*) James clearly implies that the

benefits they sought from God would soon be used up. They
would have no permanent or lasting worth. Coupled with the
word *spend* here, the word *pleasures* suggests transient grati-
fications of the wrong kind. (Contrast the more neutral use in
v 1.) No wonder they *do not receive* answers to requests of this
type!

When the last statement of v 2 is coupled with the statements of v 3, the situation becomes clearer. When James
writes, *you do not ask,* he has in mind requests which, when
answered, will meet the fundamental needs of the readers.
Among other obvious requests, they should have been asking
for peace and harmony with their brothers and an end to
turmoil in the church. But when James also writes, *you ask and
do not receive,* he has in mind misguided and undiscerning
prayer. Prayer *can* result in needs met, but it *cannot* result in
the coddling of our selfish desires. After all, God is the Giver
of *every good . . . and every perfect gift* (1:16-17). We should
be careful that the gift which we ask for suits the character of
the heavenly Giver.

**⁴Adulterers and adulteresses! Do you not know that friendship
with the world is enmity with God? Whoever therefore wants
to be a friend of the world makes himself an enemy of God.**

Exasperated as James must have been when he considered
this state of affairs (vv 1-3), it is not surprising that he breaks
forth into an exclamation that charges his readers with being
adulterers and adulteresses.[1] As in the case of "murder" (v 2),
James is probably not speaking literally. What arouses him is
the transparent infidelity to God that his readers have exhibited by craving *friendship with the world.* As will become
apparent later in the chapter, some of his readers loved to
boast about their business ventures (4:13-16). In doing so
they exhibited a crassly materialistic and *worldly* spirit.

In fact, James has already warned the readers about the need
to *keep oneself unspotted from the world* (1:27). And this
warning was immediately followed by a rebuke to behavior in
the church in which a rich person was fawned over while a

poor man was demeaned (2:1-7). What emerges from the epistle is a portrait of Christian readers, many of whom were materialistic in outlook and who cultivated connections with the wealthy, while pursuing financial success for themselves. But all of this was worldly to the core. Didn't his readers realize, James asks, that *friendship with the world is enmity with God*? Didn't they know that *whoever . . . wants to be a friend of the world makes himself an enemy of God*?

Often in the NT, the term *world* (Greek: *kosmos*) is used of a system or entity that is hostile to God and is manipulated by Satan (e.g., 1 Cor 1:20-21; 2:12; Gal 6:14; 2 Pet 1:4; 1 John 2:15-17; 3:1; 5:19). Materialism, immorality, and spiritual blindness are all components of this wicked entity and are in sharp conflict with God's interests and purposes on earth. James is insistent here (as is John in 1 John 2:15-17) that one cannot be on good terms with both God and the world. One must choose the side he is really on, and when one opts for *friendship with the world*, he automatically opts for *enmity with God*. He has chosen the status of an antagonist toward his Maker and Redeemer. It is just as when a married man decides to engage in immorality with a woman to whom he is not married. In that very decision he chooses to reject fidelity to his wife. Thus in their craving for worldly acceptance and standing, James's Christian readers have committed spiritual adultery and have renounced friendship with their Lord. It may have surprised many of them to hear it put this way, but James's aim is to wake them up to the sad depth to which their spirituality and devotion had sunk.

⁵ Or do you think that the Scripture says in vain, "The Spirit who dwells in us yearns jealously"?

And James also wants them to realize that God does not accept such infidelity with indifference. Thus he reminds them that it is not *in vain* that the *Scripture says* God's Spirit is jealous over us. This is surely the meaning of this text although no single Scripture contains exactly the words used here by James. Nevertheless, the truth that God is a *jealous*

God is well known from inspired Scripture (see e.g., Exod 20:5; 34:14; Zech 8:2). We therefore might possibly dispense with the quotation marks found in the NKJV (NT Greek had no such indicators), and we could treat James's words here as a paraphrase of biblical truth couched in terms appropriate to the NT. On the other hand, the absence from the Greek text of a word like *hoti* (that) after the word *says* leaves the impression that James is indeed quoting. In that case, the source of the quotation is unknown and might possibly be a Christian hymn or prophecy. But it would still be true that the words paraphrase what Scripture teaches and are thus quite correctly designated as something that *Scripture says*.

Yet clearly the OT truth that God is a jealous God is here combined with the NT truth that His *Spirit . . . dwells in us.*[2] But since the Holy Spirit is God, what can be said of God can also be said of the *Spirit*. If God is jealous, His Spirit is jealous. Thus James is affirming that God's indwelling Spirit *yearns jealously*[3] over the affections of his readers. He is, therefore, grieved by their pursuit of *friendship with the world*. The readers, James thinks, ought to take this most seriously, for the Scripture does not say such a thing *in vain* (i.e., lightly). If they thought so, they should reconsider promptly. In fact, the words *in vain*, coupled with the strong assertion about God's Spirit, hint at the possibility of some kind of retribution if the Spirit's yearning over them is ignored.[4]

2. Since wrath is cured by humility (4:6-5:6)

a. When it brings repentance from sin (4:6-10)

6 But He gives more grace. Therefore He says: "God resists the proud, but gives grace to the humble."

Although James has hinted at possible retribution for his readers' deplorable conduct (see v 5), he chooses not to dwell on this aspect of things. Instead, he affirms that the God whose jealousy they had aroused by desiring *friendship with the world* was nevertheless strongly inclined to be gracious. The words *He gives more grace* affirm this emphatically. God never runs out of grace—He never exhausts His supply—He always has *more grace* to give. This is surely an appropriate conclusion for this author, who had lived under the same roof with the One *full of grace and truth* (John 1:14).

In view of the inexhaustible availability of divine grace, James urges his readers to position themselves to receive it. In doing this, he quotes Prov 3:34 in the form in which that verse appeared in the Greek OT (Septuagint). If his readers remain arrogantly *proud*, God will *resist* them. Here again the hint of trouble is present. But the main point is that God *gives grace to the humble*. Divine favor (*grace*) will therefore be available to his readers if they recover the necessary attitude of humility. The rivalries and conflicts that were crippling their churches (4:1-3) were manifest expressions of pride. This spirit needed to be decisively laid aside.

⁷ Therefore submit to God. Resist the devil and he will flee from you.

What follows at this point is an unmistakable call to repentance on the part of his readers. They should begin with submission *to God*, that is, with a determination to do what is right and pleasing to Him. But as surely as they did this, Satan would test their resolve. Thus they should also *resist the devil* (just as Jesus did in His temptation), and they should expect victory over this enemy: *he will flee from you.* As great as are the powers of seduction employed by Satan, he is not invincible. A Christian firmly committed to God and the authority of His Word can rely on the help of the *Spirit who dwells* in him (v 5) and expect Satan to end his assaults and *flee* when he meets this kind of resistance.

We observe the astounding fact that this passage (specifically vv 7-10) has been called "perhaps the most comprehensive invitation to salvation in the epistles" (MacArthur, *Gospel*, p. 218). The same author goes on to say, "While James addresses most of his epistle to genuine believers, it is also evident that he is concerned about those who are not genuine." But what is there in this passage that in fact reflects

James's concern with "those who are not genuine"? The answer is: nothing at all. Such an idea is being read into a text that neither says this nor implies it. Yet, because the quoted author believes the demands mentioned here are requirements for salvation, he wrongly concludes that James is concerned with that issue. Yet, in this passage there is no call to *faith*. How can that be true if this is a "comprehensive invitation to salvation"? In addition, the Gospel of John, which calls men to eternal life in Christ (John 20:30-31), never mentions the demands specified by James, but calls repeatedly for faith and faith alone. Is John's whole Gospel, therefore, lacking in "comprehensiveness," since it nowhere mentions this kind of repentance? The travesty of making Jas 4:7-10 a Gospel passage is manifest.

⁸ Draw near to God and He will draw near to you. Cleanse your hands, you sinners; and purify your hearts, you double-minded.

But it was not enough simply to reassert one's commitment to obedience and to resisting temptation. Repentance needs to have a personal dimension in which a Christian's fractured fellowship with God is renewed. Therefore, James enjoins his readership to *draw near to God,* knowing that such action will be reciprocated: *and He will draw near to you.* Of course, as the apostle John makes clear (1 John 1:9), confession of sin is the first step in drawing near to God again. But renewed prayer and meditation on Scripture are also appropriate steps. God will respond to such steps, not only with forgiveness, but with other tokens of His nearness. He is always more eager to bridge the gap between ourselves and Him than we are. Restored closeness, therefore, between God and James's readers is precisely what James is aiming at here. God would meet them more than halfway.

As gracious as the invitation to *draw near to God* is, however, it could not be truly done apart from candid and painful renunciation of sin. When even dedicated Christians get into the Lord's presence, their wretched condition becomes acutely painful to them (see Isa 6:1-5; Rev 1:17). James's readers could hardly expect to genuinely *draw near* to God without similar feelings. Thus they are now exhorted to *cleanse* their *hands* from sin and to *purify* their *hearts* from their *double-minded* mentality. They must put away any evil thing their hands were doing. Also, they must renounce the split loyalties they had, which drew them aside to worldly concerns.

⁹ Lament and mourn and weep! Let your laughter be turned to mourning and your joy to gloom.

If this was done with discernment and with a depth of commitment, it would be natural for them to *lament and mourn and weep*. Whatever exuberance they felt should be transformed into *mourning*, and whatever delight they were experiencing must be replaced by *gloom*. This does not mean, of course, that *laughter* and *joy* are wrong. On the contrary, both are beneficial to human experience (see, e.g., Ps 126:2; Prov 17:22). However, when an individual is dealing with personal sins in the presence of God, *laughter* and *joy* are not merely inappropriate. Such levity suggests a conspicuous lack of seriousness in the repentance. But when a person's heart is moved by the depths of his wickedness in the sight of God, the responses enjoined here would seem not merely natural but also compellingly spontaneous.

The sins of which the readers needed to repent (4:1-3) fully justified the demands James makes in this verse. As in all Christian repentance, the goal was a definitive renunciation of their grievous faults. A glib and superficial repentance of sins makes the repetition of the same offenses much more likely.

¹⁰Humble yourselves in the sight of the Lord, and He will lift you up.

The objective, therefore, was a genuine humbling of themselves *in the sight of the Lord*. If they did this properly, God would someday *lift them up*. The Greek verb translated *lift . . . up* is *hypsoō* and signifies "to exalt." If the readers would now bring themselves low by repentance, God would someday "exalt" them. Whether this ever took place in this life or not, God would certainly repay their "humiliation" with an "exaltation" of His own time and choosing.

b. When it brings restraint in speech (4:11-12)

If, as James has urged, his readers adopt a true spirit of humility before God (v 10), that humility will also find expression in the way they talk about their fellow Christians.

> **¹¹ Do not speak evil of one another, brethren. He who speaks evil of a brother and judges his brother, speaks evil of the law and judges the law. But if you judge the law, you are not a doer of the law but a judge.**

Specifically, they are not to *speak evil of one another*. In congregations with the problems James has focused on (4:1-3), there could be no cessation of conflict unless there was a cessation of critical and condemning speech about others. The verb translated *speak evil (katalaleō)* is broad enough to cover any kind of negative talk that is harmful to the best interests of a Christian brother or sister, regardless of whether the subject matter was true or false (see Laws, *Epistle*, p. 186).

Such speech, of course, was also a negative judgment on the character or behavior of that fellow Christian. So James charges that the person who *speaks evil of a brother and judges his brother* was at the very same moment a person who *speaks evil of the law, and judges the law*. Here James is probably thinking once again of *the royal law* of Scripture (see 2:8) which, in Lev 19:16-18, is preceded by a warning *not to go about as a talebearer among your people* (Lev 19:16). People who went around telling others about the faults and failings of another Christian were clearly in violation of the command to *love your neighbor as yourself*. But in flouting this command by their criticisms of others, they were in effect criticizing and condemning *the royal law* itself. Since all such speech was forbidden by this law, the one who disobeyed it was virtually saying, "This law is unworthy of my obedience and I judge it to be invalid for me in this case." No doubt James's readers might be surprised by this concept, but nonetheless this was true of any and all lawbreaking. The lawbreaker was passing his own negative judgment on whatever command he disobeyed.

Such behavior was anything but humble (see v 10). Anyone who took a stance which, by its very nature, passed judgment on God's law, was placing himself *above* that law. But in that case, James says, *you are not a doer of the law but a judge.* That is, such a person has left his proper role of humble submission to *the law* and has exalted himself to the role of *a judge.* The arrogance of this, however unwittingly done, is obvious.

¹² There is one Lawgiver, who is able to save and to destroy. Who are you to judge another?

But no mere human being could fill such a role, since *there is but one Lawgiver.* God alone has power *to save and to destroy,* i.e., to preserve or take away life. The verbs used here (*sōzō* and *apollumi*) were both used very commonly in secular Greek in reference to physical life or physical death. There is no reason to read the doctrine of eternal salvation into them here. God is certainly the only One who determines our eternal destinies, but this determination is already made: believers are already free from final judgment and condemnation (John 3:18; 5:24). But here a reference to this truth is not as natural as a reference to physical life or death (as also in 1:21; 2:14; 5:15, 20). The idea will then be that though we may condemn our brothers verbally, it is God alone who determines whether *to save* them from sin's penalty of death (1:15; 5:20) or whether *to destroy* their lives as an act of chastening (cf. Acts 5:1-11; 1 Cor 11:30). (For the sense we adopt here, see Laws, *Epistle,* p. 188.)

James's "bottom line," then, is sharp and to the point: *Who are you to judge another?* If the readers' repentance (vv 7-10) is to be real, they must be humble enough to perceive their unworthiness to pass judgment on a fellow Christian. Anything else was only the fruit of arrogant self-exaltation.

c. When it brings reluctance to boast (4:13—5:6)

James has now presented his theme of humility under two categories: (1) humility in our relationship with God, and (2) humility in our speech about others. The final section on humility discusses this subject in reference to *ourselves*. In dealing with this issue, James focuses on his readers' tendency to brag about their material ambitions. But his discussion offers us significant truth about how to take a humble overview of our lives.

¹³ Come now, you who say, "Today or tomorrow we will go to such and such a city, spend a year there, buy and sell, and make a profit"; ¹⁴ whereas you do not know what will happen tomorrow. For what is your life? It is even a vapor that appears for a little time and then vanishes away.

With attention-catching abruptness, James denounces those who brag about their business plans with total disregard for the transient nature of their lives. The NKJV phrase *today or tomorrow* is read by the majority of the Greek manuscripts of James as *today and tomorrow*, and this is to be preferred. These boasters are full of self-confidence in their long-range planning. They are going to a specific city (*such and such a city*), and their journey will take them two days (*today and tomorrow*). Their plans call for *a year* of business activity there, from which they expect to *make a profit*. Yet, as James points out, these braggarts don't even *know what will happen tomorrow* (cf. Prov 27:1). They have plotted out a year's program without knowing what *tomorrow* itself may bring. Anything could take place tomorrow to frustrate their intentions. They may not even be alive tomorrow, since their lives are nothing more than *a vapor that appears for a little time and then vanishes away*.

¹⁵ Instead you ought to say, "If the Lord wills, we shall live and do this or that."

In place of being so proudly confident about their plans, they ought to recognize God's sovereign control over their business operations and even over their lifespan. What they *ought to say*, if they were truly humble, is that their lives (*we shall live*) and their activities (*do this or that*) are subject to God's will. *If the Lord wills* would have been most suitable on their lips, not as a mere formula, but as a genuine expression of their dependence on God.

¹⁶ But now you boast in your arrogance. All such boasting is evil.

But instead of this humility, the readers actually *boast in their arrogance*. This expression, however, is not altogether clear as rendered in the NKJV. The Greek phrase (*kauchasthe en tais alazoneiais hymōn*) is actually better handled by the KJV as *ye rejoice in your boastings*. We could perhaps also read it: "You glory in your proud pretensions." James's point is that the self-confident words he has just condemned (vv 13-14) were more than a lapse in their awareness of God's sovereignty. Rather, such pretentious plans were themselves a source of pride to those who announced them. That is, they loved putting these "pretensions" (*alazoneiais*) on display in order to attract the admiration of other people. Viewed in that light *such boasting* was *evil*.

How often it happens in the church that people love to lay their plans (regarding business or anything else) before men to elicit respect, admiration, and deference from others. Even a missionary or a preacher may fall into the trap of setting forth his plans for serving God as a way of obtaining honor from his fellow Christians. James's words here are a timeless reminder: *All such boasting is evil*.

¹⁷ Therefore, to him who knows to do good and does not do it, to him it is sin.

So if James's readers knew the proper way to act and speak, they should do so. For if they did not do so, their failure was itself a sin. If they knew that they should acknowledge their dependence on God's will when speaking about their plans, they should start at once to act on that knowledge, since *to him who knows to do good and does not do it, to him it is sin.* Sin, therefore, can occur not merely as a wrong act, but also as a right act which remains undone.[5] Accordingly, we dare not omit from our conversation the recognition that not only our lives, but all of our activities, are as fragile as a wisp of smoke. We must acknowledge that God alone can enable us to do whatever we hope, or plan, to do.

JAMES 5

¹ Come now, you rich, weep and howl for your miseries that are coming upon you!

At first glance the subject matter seems to have changed with this verse. But this impression ignores the fact that 4:13-17 and 5:1-6 are the only two paragraphs in James that begin with the words, *Come now.* Moreover, the theme of materialism is a solid thread uniting the two units. As we have seen, James's readers were afflicted with a severe case of worldly materialism coupled with an undue deference toward rich people (2:1-7). Their tendency to flaunt their profit-making schemes (4:13-17) was simply further evidence of their worldly outlook (see 4:4-5).

What the readers needed, therefore, was a solid and emphatic reminder of the transience of all human wealth. In order to thus remind them, James virtually dons the mantle of a prophet and speaks in terms reminiscent of OT prophecy. (See Joel 1:5, 13; Isa 13:6; 14:31; 15:3; Jer 4:8, where James's word for *howl* [*ololyzō*] occurs in the LXX, the Greek translation of these passages.) His pronouncements are obviously no longer addressed to the Christian community alone, even though the epistle was intended to be read by that community. Yet his words are designed to awaken his readers by means of a crisp announcement about the eschatological doom of all human wealth.

Looking outward at the world, then, James in prophet-like fashion announces *miseries* for the rich which ought to bring them to tears and lamentation.

² Your riches are corrupted, and your garments are moth-eaten. ³ Your gold and silver are corroded, and their corrosion will be a witness against you and will eat your flesh like fire. You have heaped up treasure in the last days.

The sorrow appropriate to the rich is now traced to the ultimate doom of all human wealth. As so often with prophetic pronouncements, a judgment yet future is presented as a *fait accompli*, and James sees human *riches* as already *corrupted*, and costly *garments* as already *moth-eaten*, and earthly *gold and silver* as already *corroded*. But then, he surprisingly adds, *their corrosion . . . will eat your flesh like fire*. This latter statement is not usually taken literally by interpreters of James, but a non-literal treatment is quite dubious.

Interpreters should take full note of the fact that in 5:1-6 James has adopted the prophetic form and is speaking in eschatological terms. We should look, therefore, for a specific fulfillment of his words, just as we do for the words of eschatological announcements elsewhere in the Scriptures. It would seem that these words fit comfortably only at one point in the Bible's prophetic perspective—namely, at the Second Advent, at the very end of the Great Tribulation. Then, but only then, will there be a definitive judgment on the human wealth of this present age. This is where the statement about *corrosion* eating men's *flesh as fire* is relevant. Actually, the word rendered *corrosion* here is *ios*, which basically means "poison" and need not refer to *corrosion* at all.

What then might this mean? Only the final fulfillment will tell us for sure, but a possibility exists that the reference could be to nuclear contamination. If Zech 14:12-15 is considered here, it appears that the *plague* which strikes the armies gathered together at Armageddon is precisely analogous to what James is saying here. The declaration by the ancient prophet that *their flesh shall dissolve while they stand on their feet, their eyes shall dissolve in their sockets, and their tongues shall dissolve in their mouths* (Zech 14:12), is striking to say the least. It could easily be fulfilled through intense exposure to atomic radiation, which would also contaminate human wealth. In that case, the gathering together of *the wealth of all the surrounding nations . . . gold, silver, and apparel in great abundance,* which Zechariah mentions (Zech 14:14), will not be for the purpose of *acquiring* that wealth but rather to *dispose* of it. The same radioactive "poison" that makes that wealth useless will also be the "poison" that eats men's *flesh like fire.*

It is hard to resist the conclusion that, when James spoke the words of vv 2 and 3, he had Zechariah's prophecy in mind. What James foresees is "poisoned" wealth which will be so useless (indeed dangerous!) that it will be allowed to corrode and decay.

This accumulation of useless wealth will stand, therefore, as a *witness against* the rich of the world since they were so foolish as to have *heaped up treasure in the last days.* The eschatological bearing of the reference to *the last days* is obvious and accords with the interpretation we are offering here.

⁴ Indeed the wages of the laborers who mowed your fields, which you kept back by fraud, cry out; and the cries of the reapers have reached the ears of the Lord of Sabaoth.

Justice will thus overtake unscrupulous wealthy men of this sinful world. Throughout history, and not only in James's day, men of wealth have often been guilty of holding back *the wages of the laborers who mowed* their *fields,* fraudulently giving them less than was right. These *wages* are here personified by James as accusers of the rich who *cry out* to God for vengeance. Moreover, these cries are heard (and will be avenged) by *the Lord of Sabaoth,* that is, by *the Lord of hosts* (Lord of armies). Here, too, the reference to the Second Advent seems plain, since our Lord will return to execute judgment riding at the head of the heavenly *armies* (see Rev 19:14).

⁵ You have lived on the earth in pleasure and luxury; you have fattened your hearts as in a day of slaughter. ⁶ You have condemned, you have murdered the just; he does not resist you.

In ancient times it was apparently customary during sheep-shearing season for men of wealth to hold a feast for which some of the sheep were slaughtered to provide meat for their festive table (see 1 Sam 25:4-8; cf. Ps 44:22; Jer 12:3). The behavior of rich men, says James, has been like that. They *have lived in pleasure and luxury,* fattening their own *hearts as in a day of slaughter.* The metaphor is vivid. Rich men are portrayed as enjoying a continual feast day, bloating their own hearts with the delights and enjoyments which were theirs in abundance. (Compare the rich man of Luke 16:19, who *fared sumptuously every day.*) Tragically, however, their *day of slaughter* was not confined to the killing of sheep. They also had *other* victims: *you have condemned, you have murdered the just* [man]; *he does not resist you.*

The hands of the rich, therefore, were stained with fraud (v 4) and murder (v 6). Righteous men, who did not resist injustice, had perished in persecutions instigated by people of wealth (see 2:6-7). The guilt of the rich was enormous. Strikingly, it is on this note of condemnation that James's prophetic oracle abruptly halts. The rhetorical impact of this sudden conclusion, however, is effective. It is as though James has pointed to the murder of just men as the final and climactic charge against the rich, which justifies everything he has foreseen for them by way of ultimate catastrophe.

Hopefully, after this dramatic denunciation of human wealth and of the wealthy, James's readers will take a lower view of the value of material things.

ENDNOTES

[1] The most used modern editions of the Greek NT (Nestle-Aland[27] and UBS[4]) read simply the word *moichalides* ("adulteresses") as over against the phrase *moichoi kai moichalides* ("adulterers and adulteresses") translated by the NKJV. The shorter reading, which is accepted by most modern translations, is almost certainly the result of a common scribal accident. This common error is called homoeoteleuton and refers to an accidental confusion of two similar syllables resulting in the omission of intervening material. Thus an early scribe might have written the syllable *moi-* (or,

moich-) of moichoi, looking down to write, and then raising his eyes and picking up the same syllable in moichalides and continuing with -chalides (or, -alides) thus omitting the intervening -choi kai moi- (or, -oi kai moich-). This would leave only moichalides ("adulteresses") as given in the majority of modern English versions.

[2] The NKJV translation, The Spirit who dwells in us, is based on accepting the reading katoikēsin instead of the reading katoikisen (read by the Nestle-Aland[27] and UBS[4] Greek texts.) The former is an aorist form of the verb katoikeō (to dwell), while katoikisen is from katoikizō (to cause to dwell). The difference is only one letter in the two forms (e in the first, which becomes i in the second), but this seemingly minor variation produces for katoikisen the translation of, for example, the NIV, "the spirit he caused to live in us." As one can notice from the lower case "spirit" in the NIV, in this alternative translation the word "spirit" is taken as a reference to man's own human spirit (a view also favored by many commentators). This view of "spirit," however, is not dependent on the textual variation since, even if we read "caused to dwell," the reference could still be to the Holy Spirit. However, in the text translated by the NKJV (and supported by a large majority of manuscripts), the reference to the Holy Spirit is even more probable. The aorist form katoikēsin is a past tense and almost means something like "has taken up residence" in us. Such a form of expression would be strange if used of the human spirit, but quite natural if used of the Holy Spirit who "took up residence" in us at the moment of our salvation.

[3] Some writers have argued that the Greek phrase pros phthonon ("unto envy," "enviously"; or, jealously as NKJV) cannot be appropriately used of God since elsewhere phthonos seems to have an unfavorable connotation. However, Martin (James, p. 150) argues to the contrary:

> But such a proposal can be countered by arguing that James may be using phthonos in this case to modify God's action. It is to be noted that the term is parallel with zēlos and that phthonos can be used interchangeably with zēlos, for both are often used for the "jealousy" of God (1 Macc 8:16; T. Sim. 4.5; T. Gad. 7.2; 1 Clem. 3.2; 4.7; 5.2). Pros phthonos [sic] can thus carry the same sense as pros zēlon (Mussner, 183). Furthermore, epipothein can have a positive connotation. The point is that James could have used phthonos instead of zēos [sic] to show that God jealously longs for his people.

The phrase "for both are often used for the 'jealousy' of God (1 Macc 8:16; T. Sim. 4.5; T. Gad. 7.2; 1 Clem. 3.2; 4.7; 5.2)" does not appear to be quite accurate and represents some kind of scholarly mishap. The references evidently should refer to places where phthonos and zēlos are used together, but not in regard to the jealousy of God (since phthonos has not been found referring to God outside of James). Still, Martin's argument can stand. If *phthonos* and *zēlos* are used together in apparently the same sense they are indeed interchangeable, and if *zēlos* can refer to divine "jealousy," as it does in the Septuagint, there is no reason why *phthonos* cannot be so used.

Davids (*Commentary*, p. 164) conjectures, "Since James has already used *zēlos* so negatively, he may deliberately select *phthonos* as a synonym not yet used."

⁴ Dibelius (*James*, p. 224) makes the same observation as we have made above at the close of v 5: "The quotation is a threat, just as we should expect after the introductory question" (i.e., after the words, *Or do you think that the Scripture says in vain*).

⁵ *The Book of Common Prayer* has this well-known confession: "We have left undone those things which we ought to have done; and we have done those things which we ought not to have done."

CHAPTER 6

Persevere in Trials to the End
(*James 5:7-20*)

V. EPILOGUE: PERSEVERANCE IN TRIALS TO THE END (5:7-20)

A. Because Perseverance Will Be Properly Rewarded (5:7-11)

It must be remembered that the overarching theme of James's letter is *testing* (1:2-21). As we saw, the admonitions of 1:19 are especially appropriate to those who were undergoing various kinds of trials. In the body of his letter, James has expounded the three commands of 1:19, while applying them to the particular needs and problems of the churches he was addressing. Now that these hortatory discussions have ended, James can return once more to the theme of trials and suffering. That he does exactly this is plain from 5:10-11, although the whole conclusion is appropriate to this theme.

⁷ Therefore be patient, brethren, until the coming of the Lord. See how the farmer waits for the precious fruit of the earth, waiting patiently for it until it receives the early and latter rain.

James's prophetic oracle (5:1-6), though really a part of the body of the epistle, nevertheless sets the stage for his conclusion. "The tension of 5:1-6 is taken up again, the day is virtually upon them" (Davids, *Commentary*, p. 184). Prophecy can be used not only to wean his readers from worldly wealth, but also to encourage them to hold out to the end, whatever trials they currently may be enduring. They need, therefore, *to be patient until the coming of the Lord.* Troubles can often heighten our anticipation of Christ's return, but if we view that return only in terms of our own pressing situation, we will be tempted to be *impatient* instead of *patient*.

In the agricultural society of Palestine in James's day, *the early and latter rain* were well known (i.e., after sowing: late autumn; before harvest: early spring). These rains were "limited to the east end of the Mediterranean" (Davids, *Commentary*, p. 183). So, *the farmer* who waited patiently for the seasonal rains which were crucial to the production of *the precious fruit of the earth* could be taken by James's Palestinian readers as a model of patience. But since the harvest image is deeply embedded in NT eschatology (e.g., Matt 13:39), there is probably also a reference here to our Lord as the divine Farmer who waits patiently for the consummation of all things. We know, in fact, on the authority of Peter, that any seeming delay in the advent of the eschatological climax (that is, *the day of the Lord*) is due to God's concern for the salvation of men (2 Pet 3:9). Thus *the precious* (i.e., "valuable") *fruit of the earth* may well refer to the full measure of conversions ordained by God to precede the Rapture of the Christian Church. Of course, the exact time at which that number will be attained is known to God alone. From our perspective, it could be reached today.

⁸ You also be patient. Establish your hearts, for the coming of the Lord is at hand.

In any case, whether one thinks of the human farmer or the divine One, James's readers can find grounds to *also be patient* and *establish* their *hearts*, since *the coming of the Lord is at hand*. In affirming this fact, however, James (like other NT writers) has been thought to be mistaken. How, it is asked, can *the coming of the Lord* have been *at hand* in James's day when over 1,950 years have passed without it having taken place? (Of course, this objection is already countered by Peter in 2 Pet 3:3-9.) There are a number of answers to this objection, which arises from unbelief, but the one that is most suitable in this context is this: the coming of the Lord is *always at hand* (Greek: *ēngike*, "has drawn near") precisely because we are not separated from it by any known event at all (see next verse). Throughout the entirety of more than 19 centuries it has always had this character so that a believer could well say, "It may be today." Anything that *must* happen, and *could* happen *today*, is in a very legitimate sense *at hand*. Thus, the readers can use this knowledge as a means of settling down and holding out, i.e., they can *establish* their *hearts*.

⁹ Do not grumble against one another, brethren, lest you be condemned. Behold, the Judge is standing at the door!

If their hearts are indeed established in this expectation, the readers will not *grumble against one another*. The word *grumble* translates a word (*stenazete*) which signifies "to groan" or "to sigh." In view of the *wars and fights* that James had earlier reproved (4:1-3), this verb sounds relatively mild by comparison. In all probability James graciously assumes that his call to repentance (4:7-12) will be heeded, and that the churches will enjoy greater internal harmony and peace. Still, however, realism called for him to caution against even the most subdued complaints of Christians against one another. Even if it was, so to speak, only a "groan" or a "sigh," they should avoid it, since the Lord's coming could take place at any time.

This sense of the imminency of the Savior's return is captured in the striking metaphor, *Behold, the Judge is standing at the door*. The readers are thereby likened to a group of litigants, or defendants, standing within a courtroom. Total silence is required out of respect for the judge who is just outside the courtroom door and about to step inside to take his place on the judgment seat. Like a Roman lictor announcing a judge's impending entry, as it were, James cries "Quiet!" His Christian readers must fully silence their complaints against one another in the realization that their Lord and Judge can at any moment appear and sit down on the Bema (Judgment Seat) in order to assess their lives (cf. 2:12-13; see also 2 Cor 5:10; Rom 14:10-12). They must therefore be careful that He does not find them nurturing a complaining spirit against their fellow believers. As Paul has so clearly stated, *So then each of us shall give account of himself to God. Therefore let us not judge one another anymore* (Rom 14:12-13a).

10 My brethren, take the prophets, who spoke in the name of the Lord, as an example of suffering and patience.

Do the readers need any additional reasons for patiently holding out to the end? If so, they can *take the prophets, who spoke in the name of the Lord* as their models. We must note here the smooth transition James makes from an admonition based on *prophecy* (the Rapture, vv 7-9) to an admonition based on *the prophets themselves.* These servants of the Lord, James is saying, knew something about *suffering and patience.* One thinks at once of men like Daniel and Jeremiah, among others.

The word translated *suffering* (*kakopatheia*) carries overtones of endurance under hardship or suffering. Thus it differs somewhat from *patience* (*makrothymia*), which signifies control of one's temper or emotions, i.e., having what is popularly called a "long (*makro-*) fuse." The readers have been told to *be patient* [Greek: *makrothymēsate*] . . . *until the coming of the Lord* (vv 7-8) and to control their temper toward each other (v 9). The prophets of old exhibited this trait of self-control all the while that they bore up under many serious trials.

11 Indeed we count them blessed who endure. You have heard of the perseverance of Job and seen the end intended by the Lord—that the Lord is very compassionate and merciful.

In the light of their sufferings, James is saying, we look back at the prophets with admiration and respect for their endurance. *Indeed,* we take the same attitude toward all who bear up well under testing: *we count them blessed who endure.* The readers could certainly say this about Job, for example, whose *perseverance* (*hypomonē*: "endurance") under trial was justly celebrated among those who honored the Hebrew Scriptures. The readers had also *seen* (in the well-known biblical story) *the end intended by the Lord.* The reference in the word *end* is clearly to the conclusion of the Book of Job, where it is stated that *the Lord blessed the latter days of Job more than his beginning* (Job 42:12). Since Job ended his days with much more than he started with, the readers could see for themselves *that the Lord is very compassionate and merciful.*

The implication of this, surely, is that the readers may expect to be "compensated" for whatever they endured (or lost) under the trials God sent their way—provided, of course, that they acquitted themselves well, as did Job and the prophets. But the general language James uses simply states that God is truly *compassionate and merciful* toward those who endure well. The readers would have no grounds for saying that their compensation must be made in material terms, as was Job's. Rather, the spiritual benefits of trials are likely to be uppermost in James's mind (cf. 1:1-12). However, in a context which so strongly points toward the coming of our Judge (vv 7-10), it is natural to think that James also had in mind the rewards that will be dispensed at the Judgment Seat of Christ (see 1 Cor 3:14; 2 Cor 5:10). Suffice it to say, James believed strongly that endurance under trial would be amply rewarded by a *compassionate and merciful* Lord.

B. Because Perseverance Can Be Undergirded by Prayer (5:12-20)

The content of 5:7-11 is tightly knit by James into a broad, general call to endure patiently until the Lord returns. It is the scriptural equivalent of songwriter Philip B. Bliss's words: "Hold the fort, for I am coming!" Now, in the concluding segment of his epistle, James gives some specific practical advice related to the readers' need to endure. As was true with the three admonitions of 1:19, so it is here. The advice given is good for all times and circumstances, but is especially relevant in times of stress and trial. James's emphasis on prayer in this section is especially noteworthy since few things undergird perseverance more effectively than prayer. In the final analysis, a persevering life is also a prayerful life.

¹² But above all, my brethren, do not swear, either by heaven or by earth or with any other oath. But let your "Yes" be "Yes," and your "No," "No," lest you fall into judgment.

First of all, he wants them to avoid oaths. *Above all (pro pantōn)* "should be viewed as an emphatic epistolary introduction" (Davids, *Commentary*, p. 189) rather than a statement elevating this command above every other command. But it is precisely when men are under stress (trials) that they are inclined to use language that is inappropriate, like swearing an oath. Peter, whom James knew well, was a classic case of this (Matt 26:74; Mark 14:71). But oaths taken to establish one's veracity in communication with others implied that one's normal affirmations were inadequate. The readers, therefore, should abstain from this kind of oath-taking. They should not *swear, either by heaven or by earth or with any other oath*, as also the Lord Himself had taught (Matt 5:34). Instead, they should be people of their word, whose simple affirmations and denials, *Yes* and *No*, were sufficient, requiring no further validation such as an oath might appear to give. Though some readers of James have extended his prohibition against oath-taking to the courtroom, it is doubtful that James has anything like that in mind. His statement appears to deal basically with our normal patterns of communication, and its application is best confined to situations where we would ordinarily make a simple affirmation or denial about something.

Furthermore, to use oaths to back up promises could easily lead to a kind of trickery by which some might technically negate the substance of an oath-bound declaration. Oath-taking was thus an open invitation to hypocrisy, that is, to a false pretense in which one carefully chose the words of his oath so that he might later find a technical reason not to fulfill them. Alternatively, oath-taking could become a mere façade behind which the truth is hidden. Such dangers seem to be in James's mind here.

The NKJV at this point renders a Greek text that means *lest you fall into* (lit. *under*) *judgment* (*hypo krisin*). But it is very likely that the few old manuscripts that contain this text reflect an ancient scribal error in which the tiny Greek word *eis* (into) has dropped out. This would leave only *hypokrisin* (hypocrisy) which editors now divide into *hypo krisin* (under judgment). A sizable majority of the Greek manuscripts of James include *eis* so that the text should read: "lest you fall into hypocrisy" (*eis hypokrisin*).

The oath-taker falls too easily into hypocrisy since it gives him the opportunity to tell lies under cover of a solemn claim to truthfulness. (Peter himself had fallen into precisely this kind of hypocrisy in his denials of the Lord.) James's wisdom amounts to this: we should never need to use an oath to prove that "this time I really mean it!" Instead we should *always* "really mean it." In this way we can avoid the trap of oath-taking, which easily allows us to plunge into hypocritical communication.

¹³ Is anyone among you suffering? Let him pray. Is anyone cheerful? Let him sing psalms.

Calmness and appropriate behavior, even under stress, are what James is really seeking here. A rash oath is a poor response to any situation. But suppose someone was really *suffering*? In that case prayer was in order. And what if someone was *cheerful*? In that case praise was in order. The word rendered *let him sing psalms* (*psalletō*) probably has the more general sense, "let him sing praise," although it is likely enough that in the early church such songs were often built on the psalms of OT Scripture.

¹⁴ Is anyone among you sick? Let him call for the elders of the church, and let them pray over him, anointing him with oil in the name of the Lord. ¹⁵ And the prayer of faith will save the sick, and the Lord will raise him up. And if he has committed sins, he will be forgiven.

In a more specific sense, what if the suffering person (mentioned in v 13) was experiencing sickness? Prayer was certainly in order (v 13), but in this case a special kind of prayer was accessible to the sick person. The sick person could *call for the elders of the church*. These men would then come and, after *anointing him with oil in the name of the Lord*, they would *pray over him*. (The Greek grammar is most naturally understood as implying that the *anointing* precedes the prayer.) Where God granted any, or all, of these men to pray a *prayer of faith*, that prayer would *save the sick* person from dying and *the Lord* would *raise him up*.

There is no real problem with this text so long as we allow it to mean what it says—and neither more nor less than it says. There is nothing here at all about a gift of healing possessed by any of *the elders*. Rather, these church leaders function simply as intercessors on behalf of the one who is *sick*. Neither does James say that recovery *always* occurs. It *will* occur where there is a *prayer of faith*, but the absence of such a prayer does not mean that the elders are spiritually deficient. It might be, in any given case, that the elders would not be at all sure whether recovery would be for the best. In such cases, they might well pray (as our Lord prayed in the Garden of Gethsemane), *"Your will be done"* (Matt 26:39-42). The more biblically based and perceptive the elders of a church are, the more readily they will be able to evaluate the specific situation in a spiritual way and to pray accordingly.

Additionally, there is no reason why the *anointing with oil* should not be carried out literally. Although this *anointing* was no doubt for symbolic purposes (a magical use of this oil is certainly *not* implied!), the symbolism is not explained by James. Since this anointing was to be done *in the name of the Lord*, at the very least we might take it to signify dependence on God's *sovereignty* over the healing process. (Shogren, *EQ*: 105, suggests the anointing was "a sign of God's healing presence.") After all, it was the sovereign *Lord* who alone could *raise* the sick person *up*. This certainly agrees with the fact that much of the anointing with oil that occurs in the OT points to God's sovereignty in choosing a person for some role (whether as prophet, priest, or king). But more than this we can hardly say, since the text is silent about the purpose behind the anointing.

It is perhaps needless to add that there is also nothing in the text which assigns the procedure described here to some other (past) dispensation. It follows that the procedure can and should be practiced today, with the proviso that (so far as James's text goes) it is the *sick* person who initiates the process, not *the elders*.

Finally, James observes that in cases where sin has occurred, forgiveness as well as healing can take place. But it is precisely the words *if he has committed sins* that serve as a necessary caution. Not all sickness is the result of sin (as some teach), but some of it is (cf. 1 Cor 11:30). The fact that someone calls for the church elders suggests that he or she is prepared to deal with any underlying sin that may have been committed. Obviously, *the elders* should make appropriate inquiries about this, unless the situation is so clear as to render inquiry unnecessary. This makes it even more plain that it may not be prudent for these church leaders to initiate the procedure James describes. If the *sick* person himself has not called them, it may well be because he has sin in his life which he is not ready to confront.

¹⁶ Confess your trespasses to one another, and pray for one another, that you may be healed. The effective, fervent prayer of a righteous man avails much.

However, all of James's readers should be prepared for that open and honest confession of sin which was a necessary prelude to healing (*that you may be healed*). But the command to *confess your trespasses to one another* is still based within James's discussion of sickness and should not be stretched into a general admonition. There is no biblical command to publicly confess all our known sins. Confession to God is necessary in regard to any sin we are aware of, and should be made in conformity with 1 John 1:9. But only here in Scripture do we find a command to make confession *to one another* and this lies fully within the parameters of our need for prayer by the elders and our fellow Christians (*pray for one another*) that God will make us well.

Hence it seems apparent that James was not thinking in vv 14-15 of instantaneous healing after the elders have prayed. Rather, he is thinking of collective prayer, both by the elders and the congregation, and he is thinking of ultimate, rather than immediate, recovery. But if the sick person has reason to believe that God's hand of discipline is upon him, he should be prepared to acknowledge his failures openly so as to clear the path for effective prayer.

Prayer *can* work wonders! Not, however, if it comes from an unrighteous heart, or if it is shallow, glib, and superficial. Rather, it *avails much* when it is an *effective, fervent prayer* expressed by *a righteous man*. The words *effective* and *fervent* both translate a single participle (*energoumenē*) which is hard to render precisely. The familiar English words used by the NKJV are on target, but since we get our verb "energize" from the Greek verb in question, we might paraphrase James's statement as "a spiritually energetic prayer" or, "a prayer energized by God." The point is that such prayer is more deeply at work in us than those which we verbalize in a casual or perfunctory state of mind, then hardly remember what we've prayed for. James is speaking of prayer that is Spirit-wrought and that comes from our heart and soul. Such prayer can be offered only by *a righteous man*, so that James implies that if the sick man will indeed turn from any sins he has committed, he could even pray effectively for himself. In fact, this is precisely what righteous King Hezekiah did in a time of near-fatal illness (2 Kgs 20:2-6), though his sickness was not related to sin as far as we know.

¹⁷ Elijah was a man with a nature like ours, and he prayed earnestly that it would not rain; and it did not rain on the land for three years and six months.

As a classic illustration of *the effectual, fervent prayer of a righteous man*, James now recalls *Elijah*, who was *a man with a nature like ours*. If his readers were tempted to think that *Elijah* was a kind of spiritual superman whose prayer life could never be reproduced, they were wrong. *Elijah* was as human as we are, yet his prayer shut up the heavens *for three years and six months*. In saying that *Elijah . . . prayed earnestly*, James uses a phrase that had its roots in a Hebrew idiom. The Greek words (*proseuchēi prosēuxato*) mean literally "with prayer he prayed," but might be paraphrased "he really prayed." The reference, as the NKJV suggests, is to the previously mentioned concept of an "effectual, fervent prayer" (v 16). James's expression here is a way of saying that it was precisely such a prayer that *Elijah* prayed. Its results spoke for themselves.

¹⁸ And he prayed again, and the heaven gave rain, and the earth produced its fruit.

Nor was this a totally isolated experience of prayer for this *righteous man*. Rather, *he prayed again* and his prayer affected both *heaven*, which *gave rain*, and *earth*, which *produced fruit*. So James is suggesting that his Christian readers, likewise, can accomplish much (see *avails much* in v 16) if they are righteous people who pray earnestly.

At this point, James has passed beyond the subject of sickness, which had launched his discussion of prayer (v 16). The healing of physical ailments was only one of the possible results of effectual prayer. As everyone who remembered the story of Elijah knew, the prayers of this prophet were instruments God used in connection with His call for repentance by His people Israel (see 1 Kings 18). The prayer that closed heaven placed Israel under God's discipline, while the prayer that opened it again brought God's blessing. But this was only after the nation had repented and turned from the worship of Baal. Thus Elijah had turned a whole nation from the error of its way (see v 20). Similar opportunities awaited the prayers James's readers could pray as well.

¹⁹ Brethren, if anyone among you wanders from the truth, and someone turns him back, ²⁰ let him know that he who turns a sinner from the error of his way will save a soul from death and cover a multitude of sins.

This truth is now made clear in the closing statement of the epistle (vv 19-20). This statement definitely must not be read in isolation from the previous discussion about prayer. James has already disclosed the fact that there could be sick people among the churches he is addressing who were guilty of sin, and that their need could be met through prayer. But there could also be others who might go spiritually astray, who might not be physically sick at all. James clearly "accepts that this need exists, and that sin remains a fact of Christian life" (Laws, *Epistle*, p. 241). So, he suggests, *if anyone . . . wanders from the truth*, any of his readers could become the person who *turns him back*, as Elijah did for Israel. It need hardly be stated by James that this could not be done without prayer. Elijah was the obvious model for such restorative endeavors.

And these endeavors were well worthwhile. In fact, anyone *who turns a sinner from the error of his way* (*hodos*: "road") is in reality turning him aside from a sinful path that can lead him to his physical death (see 1:15). Thus a Christian's efforts for the restoration of his brother to the pathway of obedience are life-saving in scope. If successful, he *will save a soul* (*psychē*: "life," "person") *from death*. But he will do more than that, since a restored sinner receives the gracious forgiveness of God. Thus the many sins created and multiplied by a man who turns away from God are all removed from view when that man turns back to God. The word rendered *cover* here (*kalyptō*) means "conceal." The restored sinner's *multitude of sins* are now out of sight through the pardon he has received. And the loving brother who turns him back is credited not only with the preservation of his fellow Christian's life, but also with making him clean, as if his efforts have removed from view all the unsightly moral disfigurements which sin creates. (Though, of course, only the Lord actually cleanses anyone.) Thanks to such personal involvement, the formerly erring Christian is both physically alive and spiritually clean.

And here the epistle ends. But in no sense is this ending flat or anticlimactic. On the contrary, in his impressive conclusion (5:7-20), James has carried his readers all the way from a state of grumbling against each other (v 9), to a loving mutual concern for one another's physical needs (see v 16), to the highest point of all: concern about a brother's sin (vv 19-20). When we have reached this plateau, we have indeed surmounted our self-centered concern for our own trials and testings. We now have our eyes focused on the spiritual needs of our brothers and sisters, our hearts lifted in prayer for them, and our hands outstretched to draw them back into the right road.

When all of that is true of us, our conduct will be worthy of our coming King because we are obedient to His *royal law* (2:8): *"You shall love your neighbor as yourself."*

ABBREVIATIONS
AND BIBLIOGRAPHY

LIST OF ABBREVIATIONS

BGD   Bauer, Gingrich, and Danker. *A Greek-English Lexicon*
                of the New Testament and Other Early Christian Literature

BibSac   *Bibliotheca Sacra*

CBQ   *Catholic Biblical Quarterly*

ChHist   *Church History*

EQ   *Evangelical Quarterly*

ET   *Expository Times*

GTJ   *Grace Theological Journal*

HE   *Historia Ecclesiastica (Ecclesiastical History):* Eusebius of
                Caesarea (ca. A.D. 260 – ca. A.D. 340)

HTR   *Harvard Theological Review*

JB   *Jerusalem Bible*

JBL   *Journal of Biblical Literature*

KJV   The King James Version of the Bible

LXX   The Septuagint (Greek OT)

MM   Moulton and Milligan. *The Vocabulary of the Greek New*
                Testament Illustrated from the Papyri and Other
                Non-Literary Sources

NASB	The New American Standard Bible
Nestle-Aland [27]	Nestle-Aland's *Novum Testamentum Graece*, 27th edition
NIV	The New International Version of the Bible
NKJV	The New King James Version of the Bible
NTS	*New Testament Studies*
RevExp	*Review and Expositor*
RSV	The Revised Standard Version of the Bible
UBS[4]	The United Bible Society's Greek NT, 4th Edition
ZNW	*Zeitschrift für die Neutestamentliche Wissenschaft*

Note: When we refer to books and commentaries in the text, we give the author's last name, an abbreviated title, and the page number(s). When referring to journal articles, we give the author's last name, an abbreviation of the name of the journal, and the page number(s). The reader then must consult the Bibliography for full bibliographic details on all references.

BIBLIOGRAPHY

I. Commentaries and Books

Adamson, James B. *The Epistle of James*. Grand Rapids: Eerdmans, 1976. Conservative but limited in value.

(BGD) *A Greek-English Lexicon of the New Testament and Other Early Christian Literature*. Trans. and adapted from the fourth revised and augmented edition of Walter Bauer's *Griechisch-Deutsches Wörterbuch zu den Schriften des Neuen Testaments und der übrigen urchristlichen Literatur* by William F. Arndt and F. Wilbur Gingrich, 2nd ed. rev. and augmented by F. Wilbur Gingrich and Frederick W. Danker from Walter Bauer's 5th ed., 1958. Chicago: University of Chicago Press, 1979.

Calvin, John. *Commentaries on the New Testament*. Edited by D. W. and T. F. Torrance. Edinburgh, 1959-1972.

Cantinat, Jean. *Les Épîtres de Saint Jacques et Saint Jude*. Paris: J. Gabalda, 1973.

Dale, R. W. *The Epistle of James and Other Discourses*. London: Hodder and Stoughton, 1895. Old, Calvinistic.

Darby, John Nelson. *Synopsis of the Books of the Bible*. Vol. 5: Colossians—The Revelation. Reprint ed.: Kingston-on-Thames: Stow Hill Bible and Tract Depot, 1949.

Davids, Peter H. *The Epistle of James: A Commentary on the Greek Text*. Grand Rapids: Eerdmans, 1982. Very current, properly concerned with the structure of James.

_____. *James*. Peabody, MA: Hendrickson, 1989. More recent, abbreviated version of previous entry.

Dibelius, Martin. *James*. Rev. by Heinrich Greeven. Trans. by Michael A. Williams. Ed. by Helmut Koester. Philadelphia: Fortress Press, 1976. Authorship gives this volume considerable prestige. Limited by form-critical approach.

Hodges, Zane C. *Dead Faith—What Is It? A Study of James 2:14-26*. Dallas: Redención Viva, 1987.

_____. *The Gospel Under Siege: Faith and Works in Tension*. 2nd ed. Dallas: Redención Viva, 1992.

_____. *Grace in Eclipse: A Study on Eternal Rewards*. 2nd ed. Dallas: Redención Viva, 1987.

Hort, F. J. A. *The Epistle of St. James: The Greek Text with Introduction, Commentary as far as Chapter IV, Verse 7, and Additional Notes*. London: MacMillan, 1909. Reprinted in *Expository and Exegetical Studies, Compendium of Works Formerly Published Separately by the Late F.J.A. Hort*. Minneapolis: Klock & Klock Christian Publishers, 1980. Hort never finished this commentary, but it exhibits his distinctive and idiosyncratic approach.

Johnstone, Robert. *Lectures Exegetical and Practical on the Epistle of James*. 2nd ed. Edinburgh: Oliphant, Anderson and Ferrier, ca. 1888. Old, Calvinistic.

Kennedy, George A. *New Testament Interpretation through Rhetorical Criticism*. Chapel Hill, NC: University of North Carolina Press, 1984. Clear introduction to rhetorical criticism. Liberal.

Knowling, R. J. *The Epistle of St. James*. London: Methuen, 1904. Limited value because information is outdated.

Laws, Sophie. *A Commentary on the Epistle of James*. San Francisco: Harper & Row, 1980. Liberal but current and useful.

MacArthur, John F., Jr. *The Gospel According to Jesus*. Grand Rapids: Zondervan, 1988.

Martin, Ralph P. *James*. Waco, TX: Word Books, 1988. Part of the Word Biblical Commentary series. Current but technical.

Mayor, Joseph B. *The Epistle of St. James: The Greek Text with Introduction, Notes, Comments and Further Studies in the Epistle of St. James*. 3rd ed. London: MacMillan, 1913. Reprint ed.: Minneapolis: Klock & Klock Christian Publishers, 1977. Old but contains helpful material hard to find elsewhere.

Mitton, C. Leslie. *The Epistle of James*. Grand Rapids: Eerdmans, 1966. Superior modern exegetical commentary.

Moo, Douglas J. *The Letter of James: An Introduction and Commentary*. Grand Rapids: Eerdmans, 1985. Replaces Tasker's volume (see below) in The Tyndale New Testament Commentary series. Brief, competent, but a bit behind the curve on structural analysis.

Motyer, J. A. *The Message of James: The Tests of Faith*. Downers Grove, IL: Inter-Varsity Press, 1985. Interesting for its structural suggestions, but—as title indicates—typically Reformed theological approach.

Moulton, James Hope, and Milligan, George E. *The Vocabulary of the Greek Testament Illustrated from the Papyri and Other Non-Literary Sources*. Grand Rapids: Wm. B. Eerdmans, 1960.

Plummer, Alfred. *The General Epistles of St. James and St. Jude*. New York: A. C. Armstrong and Son, 1905.

Robertson, A. T. *Studies in the Epistle of James*. Revised and edited by Heber F. Peacock. Nashville: Broadman Press, n.d. Helpful work by a well-known Southern Baptist grammarian and scholar.

Robinson, John A. *Redating the New Testament*. Philadelphia: Westminster Press, 1976. An ultra-liberal who offers conservative dates for the NT books!

Ropes, James Hardy. *A Critical and Exegetical Commentary on the Epistle of St. James*. Edinburgh: T & T Clark, 1916. Although old, a good technical commentary.

Tasker, R.V.G. *The General Epistle of James*. Grand Rapids: Eerdmans, 1956. Conservative but brief.

Vouga, François. *L' Épître de Saint Jacques*. Geneva: Labor et Fides, 1984.

II. Periodical Articles

Achtemeier, Paul J. "*Omne Verbum Sonat:* The New Testament and the Oral Environment of Late Western Antiquity," *Journal of Biblical Literature* 109 (1990): 3-27. An important discussion of the oral aspects of the NT books.

Amphoux, C. B. "Systèmes anciens de division de l' épître de Jacques et composition littéraire," *Biblica* 62 (1981): 390-400. Discusses the structure of James.

Donker, Christiaan E. "Der Verfasser des Jak und sein Gegner: Zum Problem des Einwandes in Jak 2 18-19," *Zeitschrift für die Neutestamentliche Wissenschaft* 72 (1981): 227-40. A discussion of the problem of the objector which takes James 2:18-19 as the words of one speaker.

Francis, Fred O. "The Form and Function of the Opening and Closing Paragraphs of James and 1 John," *Zeitschrift für die Neutestamentliche Wissenschaft* 61 (1970): 110-26. A seminal study helpful for the structure of James.

Fry, Euan. "Commentaries on James, 1 and 2 Peter, and Jude," *Bible Translator* 41 (1990): 326-36. Addresses the structure of James.

_____. "The Testing of Faith. A Study of the Structure of the Book of James," *Bible Translator* 29 (1978): 427-35. A structural study.

Geyser, A. S. "The Letter of James and the Social Condition of His Addressees," *Neotestamentica* 9 (1975): 25-33. An analysis of the structure of James in light of its readership.

Hayden, Daniel R. "Calling the Elders to Pray," *Bibliotheca Sacra* 138 (1981): 258-66. A recent view of this problematic passage.

Heide, Gale Z. "The Soteriology of James 2:14," *Grace Theological Journal* 12 (1991): 69-98. An effort to counter the grace view of James 2.

Hiebert, D. Edmond. "The Unifying Theme of the Epistle of James," *Bibliotheca Sacra* 135 (1978): 221-31. Representative of the view of James that is traditional in many circles.

Hodges, Zane C. "Light on James Two from Textual Criticism," *Bibliotheca Sacra* 120 (1963): 341-50.

Howard, George. "Was James An Apostle?" *Novum Testamentum* 19 (1977): 63-64. Response to an article that claimed James was not an apostle.

Jacobs, Irving. "The Midrashic Background for James II. 21-3," *New Testament Studies* 22 (1976): 457-64.

Johanson, Bruce C. "The Definition of 'Pure Religion' in James 1[27] Reconsidered," *Expository Times* 84 (1973): 118-19.

Johnson, Luke Timothy. "James 3:13-4:10 and the *Topos Peri Phthonou*," *Novum Testamentum* 25 (1983): 327-47. Provocative discussion with extensive reference to Hellenistic philosophy and Hellenistic-Jewish materials.

_____. "The Mirror of Remembrance (James 1:22-25)," *Catholic Biblical Quarterly* 50 (1988): 632-45. Helpful on this passage.

_____. "The Use of Leviticus 19 in the Letter of James," *Journal of Biblical Literature* 101 (1982): 391-401. A thesis worth careful consideration.

Kee, Howard Clark. "The Changing Meaning of Synagogue: A Response to Richard Oster," *New Testament Studies* 40 (1994): 281-83.

Lodge, John G. "James and Paul at Cross-Purposes? James 2:22," *Biblica* 62 (1981): 195-213.

Lorenzen, Thorwald. "Faith without Works does not count before God! James 2[14-26]," *Expository Times* 89 (1978): 231-35. Challenges efforts to harmonize James and Paul.

Maier, Paul L. "Sejanus, Pilate, and the Date of the Crucifixion," *Church History* 37(1968): 3-13. A convincing study.

Marconi, Gilberto. "La struttura di Giacomo 2," *Biblica* 68 (1987): 250-57. Detailed analysis of James 2.

Nicol, W. "Faith and Works in the Letter of James," *Neotestamentica* 9 (1975): 7-24.

Shogren, Gary S. "Will God Heal Us—A Re-Examination of James 5:14-16a," *Evangelical Quarterly* 33 (1989): 99-108. Worthwhile study.

Songer, Harold S. "Introduction to James," *Review and Expositor* 83 (1986): 357-68. Adopts the view that James (whoever he was!) wrote a paraenetic (ethical) treatise.

van der Westhuizen, J.D.N. "Stylistic techniques and their functions in James 2:14-26," *Neotestamentica* 25 (1991): 89-107. An application of rhetorical criticism to James 2.

Wall, Robert W. "James as Apocalyptic Paraenesis," *Restoration Quarterly* 32 (1990): 11-22. Recent survey of issues in the study of James.

Ward, R. B. "Partiality in the Assembly," *Harvard Theological Review* 62 (1969): 87-97.

Watson, Duane F. "James 2 in Light of Greco-Roman Schemes of Argumentation," *New Testament Studies* 39 (1993): 94-121. Shows continuing impact of rhetorical criticism upon the study of James.

Made in the USA
Las Vegas, NV
14 April 2023

70582045R00072